Artur Juszczak

Republic
P-47 Thunderbolt "Bubbletop"

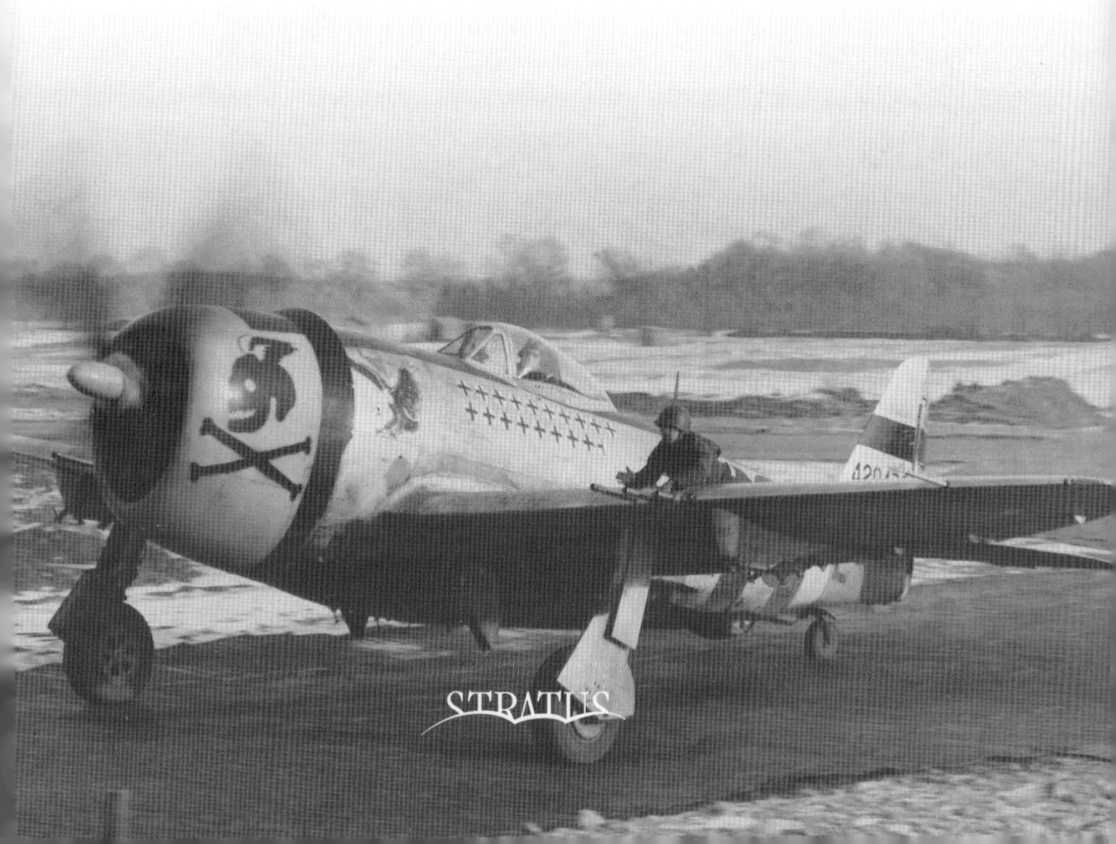

STRATUS

Published in Poland in 2011
by STRATUS s.c.
Po. Box 123,
27-600 Sandomierz 1, Poland
e-mail: office@mmpbooks.biz
for
Mushroom Model Publications,
3 Gloucester Close, Petersfield,
Hampshire GU32 3AX, UK.
e-mail: rogerw@mmpbooks.biz

http://www.mmpbooks.biz

ISBN
978-83-61421-27-6

Editor in chief
Roger Wallsgrove

Editorial Team
Bartłomiej Belcarz
Artur Juszczak
James Kightly
Robert Pęczkowski

DTP
Robert Pęczkowski
Artur Juszczak

Colour Drawings
Artur Juszczak

Scale Plans
Dariusz Karnas

Printed by:
Drukarnia Diecezjalna,
ul. Żeromskiego 4,
27-600 Sandomierz
tel. (15) 832 31 92;
fax (15) 832 77 87
www.wds.pl marketing@wds.pl

PRINTED IN POLAND

Photo: Tomasz Kantorowicz

Pamięci Szymka poświęcam.
In memory of Szymek.
Szymon Siwielec
1966-2010

Acknowledgements:
Author wish to acknowledge the kind assistance of the following:
Piotr Wiśniewski, Przemysław Skulski, George Papadimitriou, Mikael Orlog, James Kightly, Tomasz Kopański, Guilherme Furtado Filho, Álvaro Romero, Jorge Delgado, Jim Sterling, Paweł Przymusiała, Bohumil Kudlicka, Chris Barne, MAP, Kenneth Kik – www.368thfightergroup.com, US National Archives.

Get in the picture!

Do you have photographs of historical aircraft, airfields in action, or original and unusual stories to tell? MMP would like to hear from you! We welcome previously unpublished material that will help to make MMP books the best of their kind. We will return original photos to you and provide full credit for your images. Contact us before sending us any valuable material: ***rogerw@mmpbooks.biz***

Table of contents

Introduction 4
P-47D-25-RE 5
P-47D-26-RA 12
P-47D-27-RE 12
P-47D-28-RA/RE 12
P-47D-30-RA/RE 16
P-47D-40-RA 20
YP-47M 21
P-47M-1-RE 21
XP-47N 22
P-47N-1 22
P-47N-5 22
P-47N-2 27
P-47N-15 27
P-47N-20-RE and RA 27
P-47N-25 27
F-47D and N 28
TECHNICAL DESCRIPTION 31
P-47 Thunderbolt 'Bubbletop' specification 35
Thunderbolt II 37
Other Foreigner Users 38
Bibliography 40
Detail photos 41
General view 41
Fuselage 47
Wing 56
Canopy 63
Cockpit 68
Tail 88
Engine 93
Undercarriage 106
Armament 117
Colour profiles 129

Title page: *P-47D-30-RE Thunderbolt, s/n 44-20473 of 353rd FS, 354th FG, 9th AF. This plane was usually flown by Maj. Glenn Eagleston, the commanding officer of the 353rd FS. Eagleston was the top ace of the 9th AF with 18.5 victories. The crewman riding on the wing was there to help guide the plane on the taxiways because the pilots couldn't see past the nose.*

(US National Archives)

Introduction

The Republic P-47 Thunderbolt was the largest and heaviest single-seat, single-engine fighter of WW2. It incorporated the largest engine then available, the P&W R-2800, allied to a turbosupercharger, and the heaviest armament carried by any wartime US single-seat fighter. Despite its weight and bulk it was an effective fighter in air-to-air combat, and its long range potential and good weapons-carrying abilities made it an effective and valued warplane over Europe and in the Far East from its service introduction in early 1943. It served with the USAAF, RAF, Brazilian and French forces during WW2, and with many other users post-war. Despite being partly replaced by the P-51 Mustang as the war progressed, the P-47 can be credited with a major role in defending the 8th AF bombers over Europe and taking the fight to the Luftwaffe. Indeed, the top-scoring fighter unit of the USAAF in Europe (56th FG) retained its T'Bolts to the end of the conflict, and boasted the top-scoring pilot in Francis Gabreski (31 kills - *including aircraft destroyed on the ground.*). In the crucial period of mid-1943 to mid-1944 the P-47D was the 8th AF's main escort fighter, in the thick of the bitter fighting over Occupied Europe.

The story of this great warplane has been told many times. In this book we are concentrating on the technical specification and colours of the later "bubble-top" P-47D/M/N variants.

Since the Thunderbolt first entered operational use in 1943, the most common complaint from its pilots was poor visibility from the cockpit. A makeshift solution to this was to fit blown hoods, manufactured in Britain. However, this modification was never introduced onto the production line. Engineers from the Farmingdale plant attempted to cure this problem by re-shaping the entire upper fuselage, following the pattern of the

P-47D-25-RE, s/n 42-26459, SX-Z, 'Eager Eddie' of 353rd FG, 352nd FS.

(US National Archives)

Hawker Typhoon. In the summer of 1943 the P-47D-5-RE serial no. 42-8702 had its rear fuselage modified, and a tear-drop shaped hood fitted. Also the windscreen was redesigned, with the bullet-proof panel fitted as an integral part. The sliding hood was fitted with an electric actuator. In emergency the hood could be jettisoned. The converted aeroplane was designated the XP-47K. Similar modifications were also made to another 'razorback': P-47D-20-RE no. 42-76614, this machine also receiving an R-2800-59 engine. This aeroplane was designated the XP-47L. Although not built in series, it was the forerunner of the production 'bubbletop' version.

P-47D-25-RE

First production 'bubbletop' versions were built by the Republic Farmingdale plant. The tear-drop shaped hood and reduced-height upper rear fuselage spine were similar to those of the XP-47K and L. Apart from that the machines were similar to the D-22-RE. This variant was powered by a Pratt & Whitney R-2800-59 injection engine with a turbo-supercharger controlled by the General Electric A-23 regulator. The engine drove a Hamilton Standard Hydromatic 24E50-65 propeller. This batch was fitted with internal fuel tanks enlarged from 305 to 370 gallons, and the tank for the water injected into the engine was enlarged to 30 gallons, extending the increased boost operation time for the engine. Cockpit arrangements were also altered.

Apart from the standard armament of eight 0.5 in. Browning machine guns, this version of the Thunderbolt featured five external hardpoints: two under each wing and one under the fuselage, to carry bombs or fuel tanks. Additionally, a triple M-10 Bazooka rocket launcher could be fitted under each wing.

A total of 385 P-47D-25-REs were built at Farmingdale.

P-47D-25-RE, s/n 42-26428, (in the foreground) in flight before delivery to combat unit.
(Smithsonian Institution via P. Skulski)

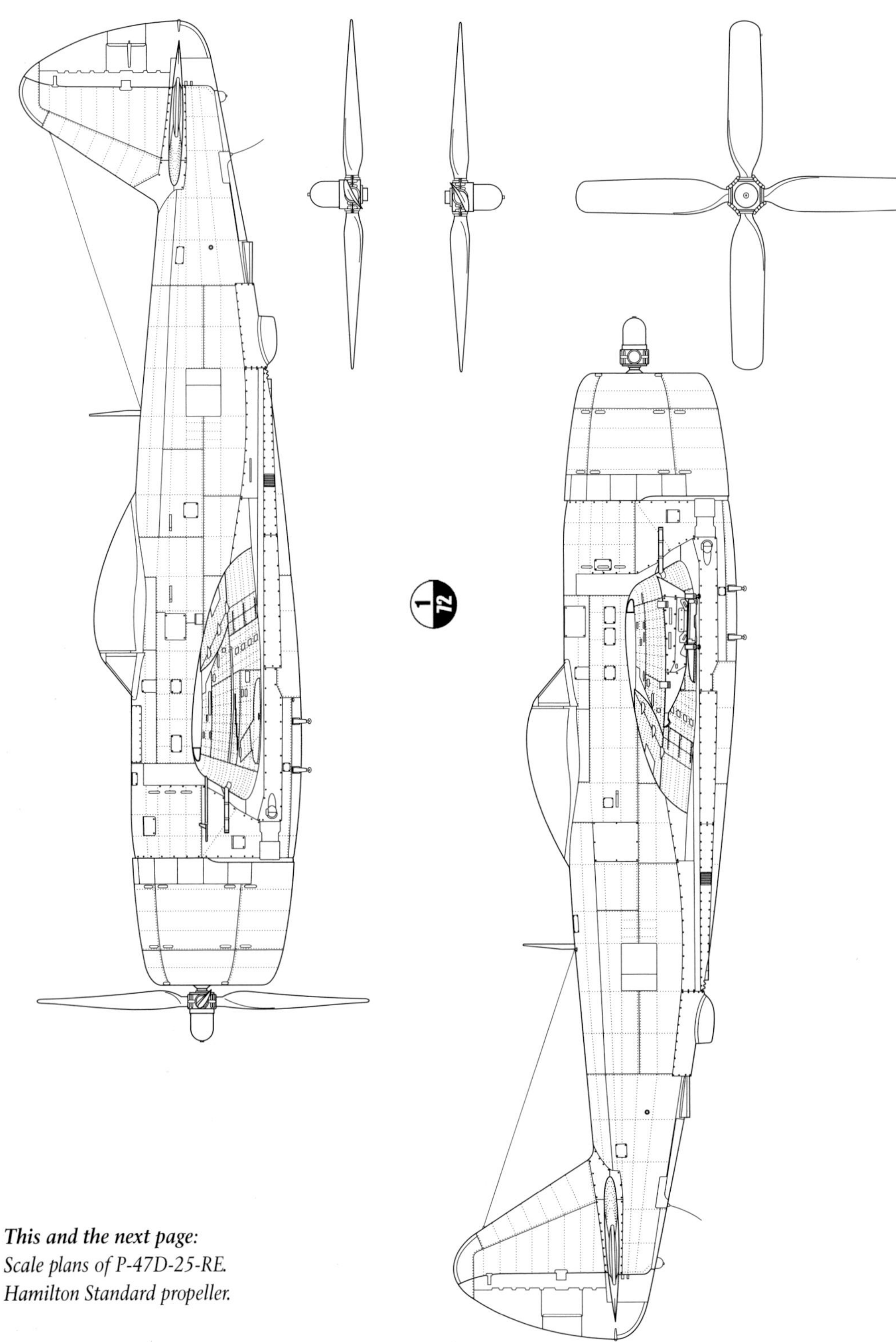

This and the next page:
Scale plans of P-47D-25-RE.
Hamilton Standard propeller.

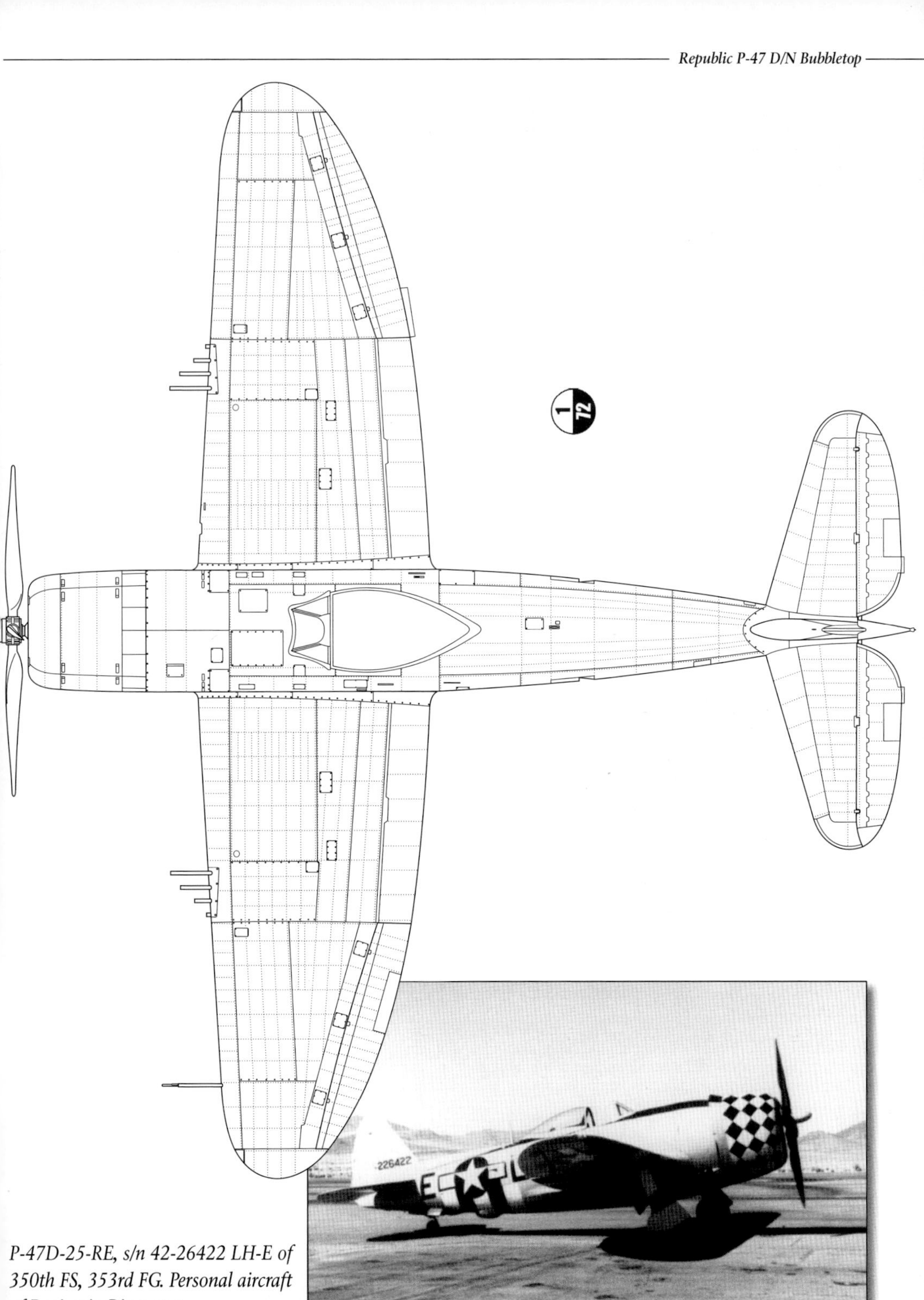

P-47D-25-RE, s/n 42-26422 LH-E of 350th FS, 353rd FG. Personal aircraft of Benjamin Rimerman.
(US National Archives)

This and the next page:
Scale plans of P-47D-25-RE.
Hamilton Standard propeller.

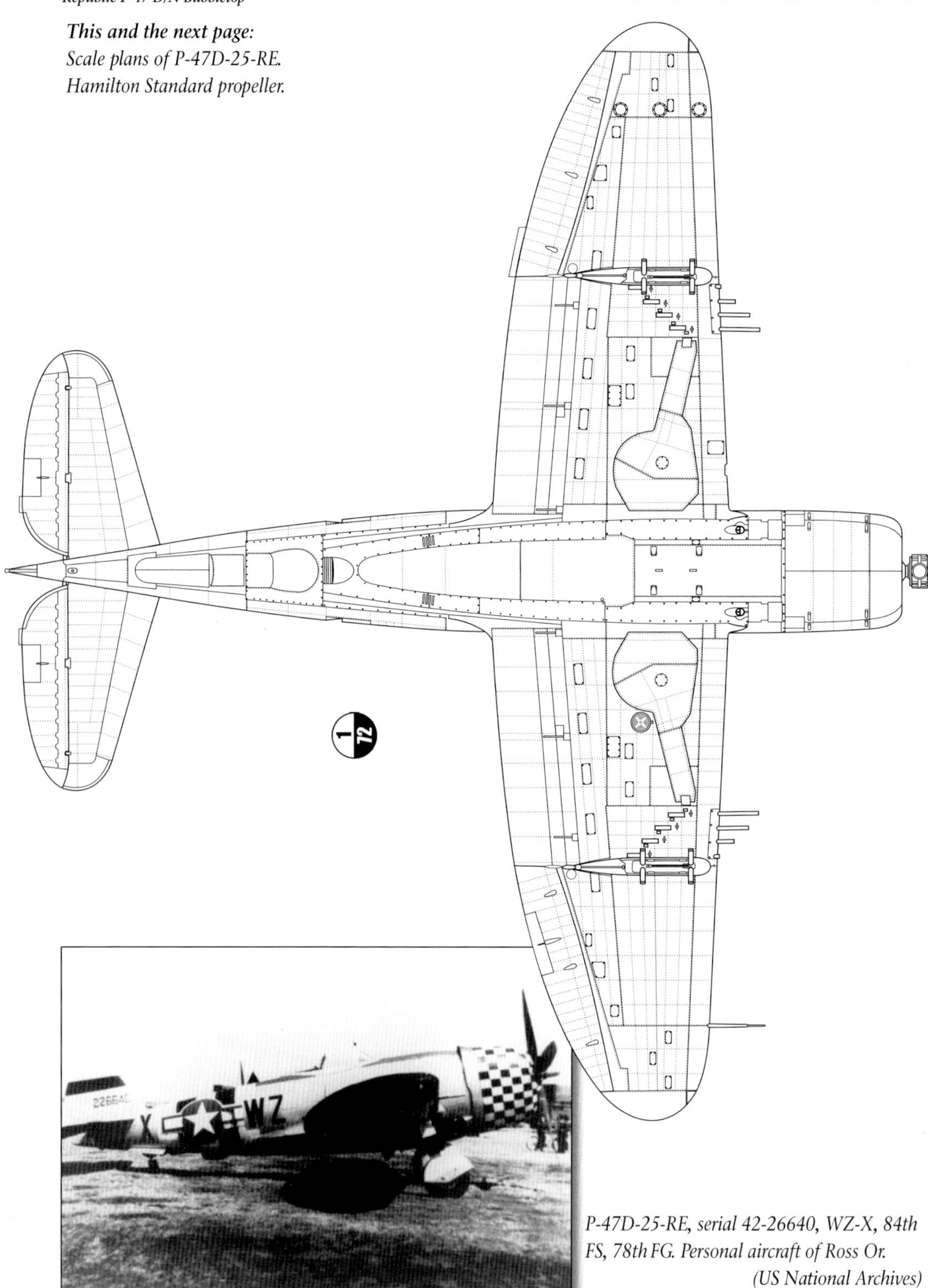

P-47D-25-RE, serial 42-26640, WZ-X, 84th FS, 78th FG. Personal aircraft of Ross Or.
(US National Archives)

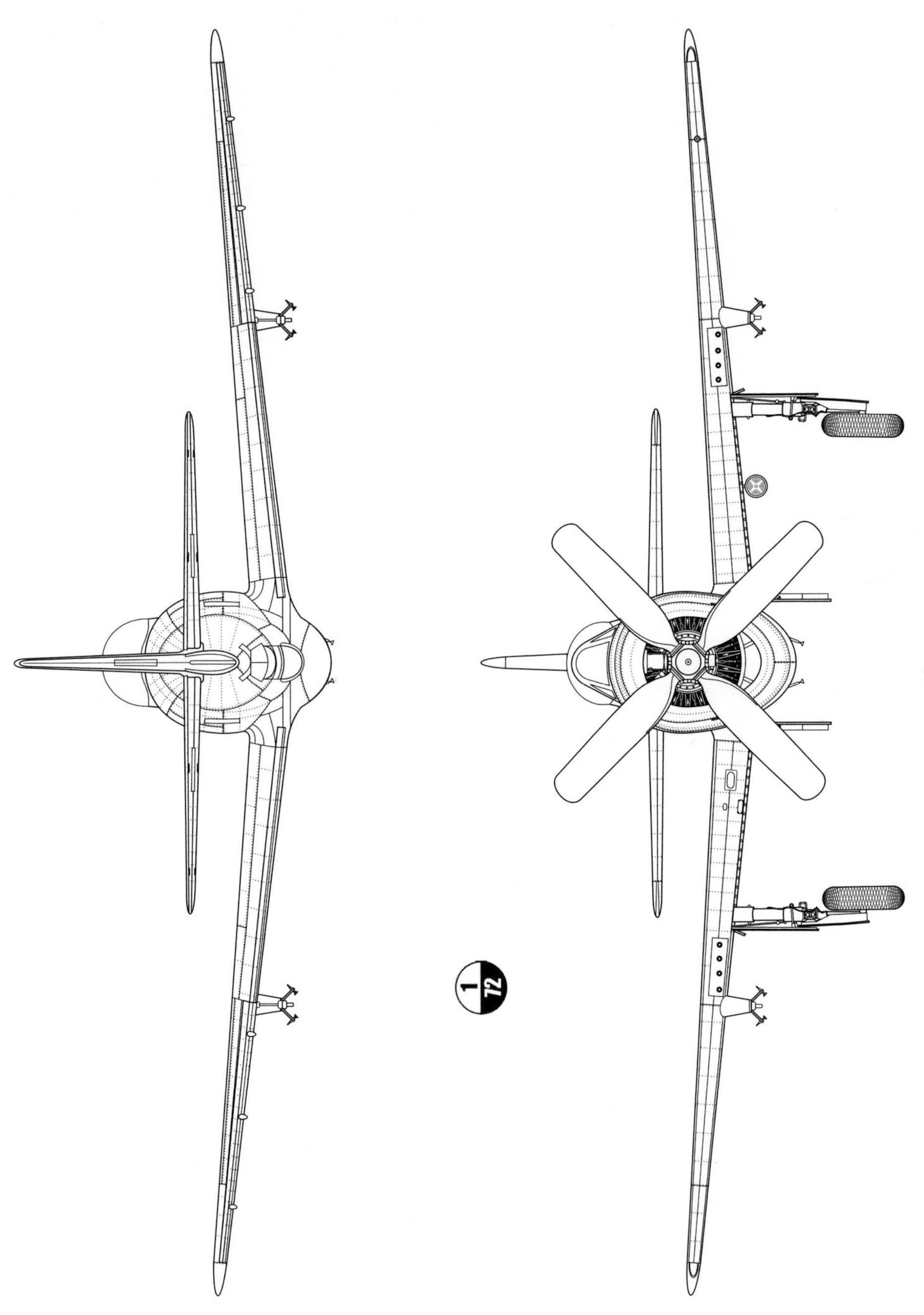
1
72

P-47D-25-RE, s/n 42-26688, U9-K of 373rd FS, 411th FG, pilot Capt. Edmund G. King.

(US National Archives)

Side view *of P-47D-25-RE. with undercarriage in open position and fuel tank under fuselage.*

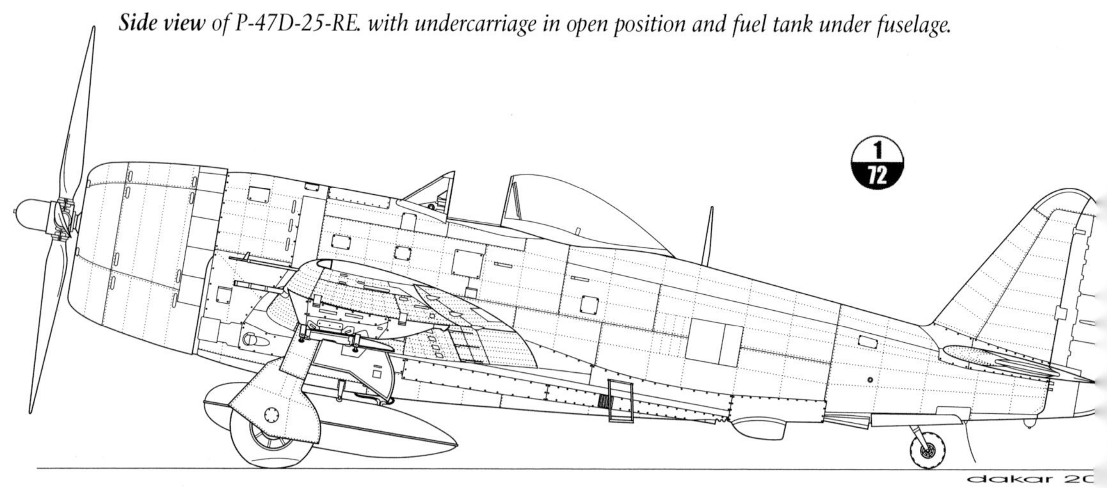

Above: *P-47D-25-RE, s/n: 42-26637 VX-P, "Kokomo" of VIII Fighter Command, 8th AF, USAAF Pilot - CO of VIII Fighter Command Gen.Maj.William Kepner. Bushey Hall, UK, 1944.*

(US National Archives)

Below: *P-47D-25-RE, s/n 42-26459 SX-Z. Lt. Edward C. Andrews of the 352nd FS, 353rd FG with his ground crew. The aircraft had been previously assigned to 352nd commander Ltc Bill Bailey and coded SX-B.*

(US National Archives)

P-47D-26-RA

This version was built by the Republic subsidiary at Evansville, and differed from Farmingdale-built D-25s only in the propeller: Curtiss Electric C542S-A114.

A total of 250 P-47D-26-RAs were built.

P-47D-27-RE

This was a modified D-25 built at Farmingdale. The most important change was the improved water injection system of the engine, which increased its output by 130 hp. Moreover, the ignition system and the external fuel tank plumbing were modified.

A total of 611 P-47D-27-REs left Farmingdale.

P-47D-28-RA/RE

This batch was manufactured by the two plants: both Evansville - and Farmingdale-built machines featured Curtiss Electric C542S propellers. Additionally, the cockpit control layout was altered and a radio direction finder was added.

The two plants produced a total of 1,778 Thunderbolts in this variant.

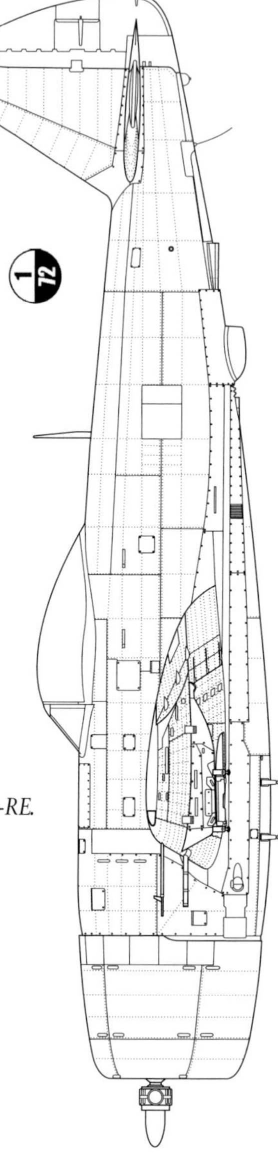

Right: *Side view of P-47D-28-RE.*

Left: *P-47, s/n unknown but probably D-27 version, "#78" of the 66th FS, 57th FG "Puny Pug".*

(J. Sterling)

Right: *Curtiss Electric C542S-A114 proppeler.*

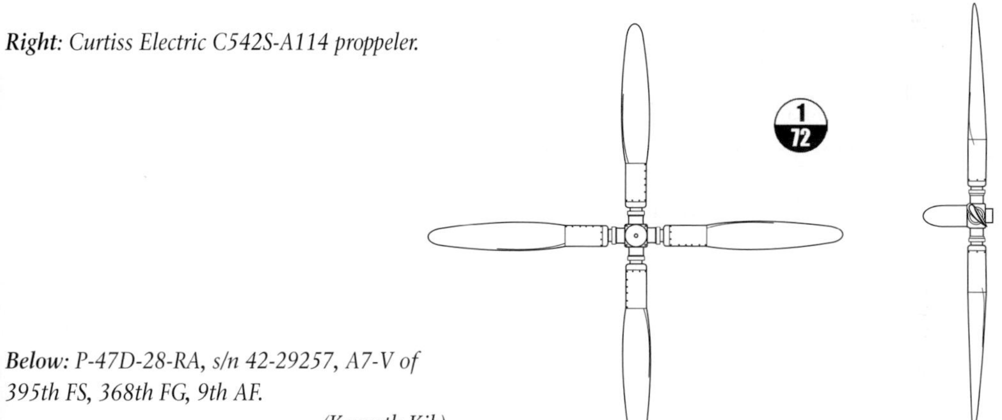

Below: *P-47D-28-RA, s/n 42-29257, A7-V of 395th FS, 368th FG, 9th AF.*

(Kenneth Kik)

P-47D-28-RA, s/n 42-28830, A7-Y, of 395th FS, 368th FG, 9th AF. (Kenneth Kik)

P-47D-27-RE, s/n. 42-27339, MX-S, 82nd FS, 78th FG.. Personal aircraft of Lt. Col. Joseph E. Myers.
(US National Archives)

Two photos of P-47D-27-RE, serial 42-26960, '69', "The Ox Cart" of 65th FS, 57th FG (12 AF)
(Smithsonian Institution via P. Skulski)

Above: P-47D-28-RE, s/n 44-20244, CP-J, of 358th FS, 367th FG.

(US National Archives)

***Below**: P-47D-28-RE, s/n 44-19566 of82nd FS, 78th FG, 8th AF. This plane had two different assigned pilots and two different names while serving with the 78th FG. Lt.Col. Jack J. Oberhansley was the C.O. of the 82nd Fighter Squadron and named the plane "Iron Ass". Col. Benjamin I. Mayo was the 78th Fighter Group's C.O. and named the plane "No Guts - No Glory".*

(US National Archives)

P-47D-30-RE, serial 44-20978, '603', "TORRID TESSIE / PHILADELPHIA FILLY" of FS 346th, 350th FG. Personal aircraft of Charles E. Gilbert. Note that aircraft has the dorsal fin installed.

(US National Archives)

P-47D-30-RA/RE

This version introduced a number of important changes. The aircraft were fitted with additional compressibility flaps to assist dive recovery. Also the ailerons were modified with a blunt leading edge, this improving high speed control. The rear-view mirror was repositioned inside the cockpit, attached to the windscreen framing. The spare optical gun sight was removed from the forward fuselage. Under-wing pylons were fitted permanently and an electric release system for the external stores was fitted. Aircraft built at Evansville featured Curtiss Electric C642S-B propellers. A change that was less noticeable externally was that the cockpit floor was now smooth, having been corrugated previously. In service most aircraft were retro-fitted with dorsal fillets.

This was the most numerous 'bubbletop' version: a total of 2,600 were built.

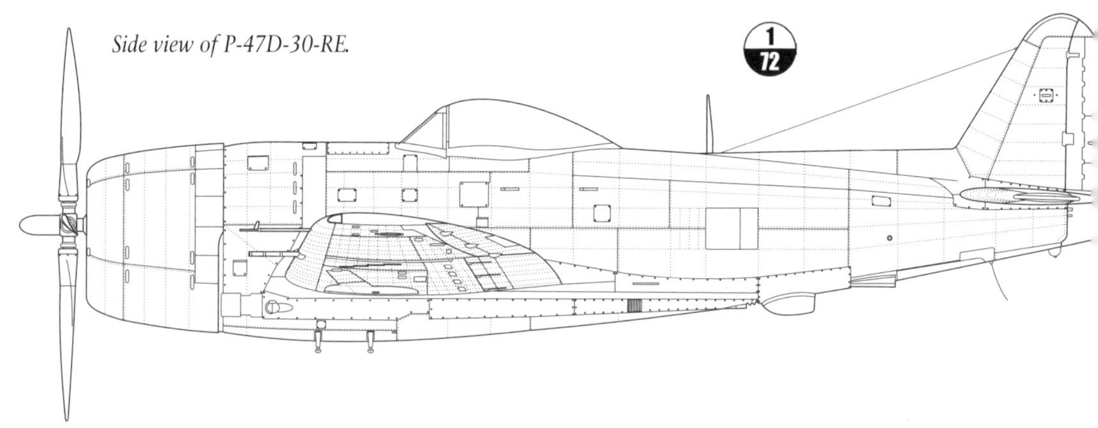

Side view of P-47D-30-RE.

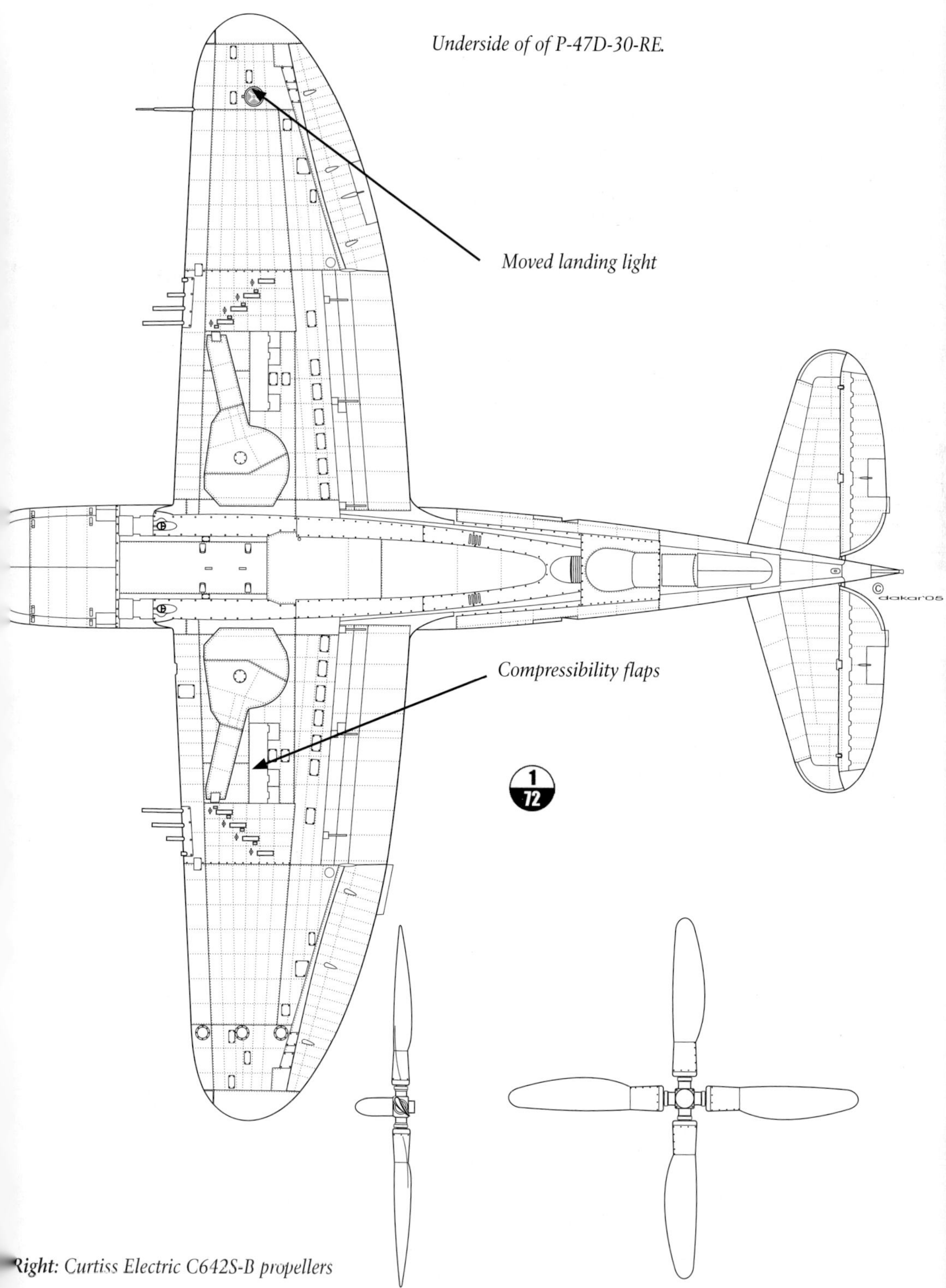

Right: Curtiss Electric C642S-B propellers

P-47D-30-RE, Thunderbolt II of 60 Squadron, the last RAF squadron converted to Thunderbolts in June 1945. This squadron operated against Indonesian nationalist guerrillas in Java, late 1945.

(Stratus coll.)

P-47D-30-RE, s/n 44-90219, 'TEST PE219' used after the war as a test bed.

(Smithsonian Institution via P. Skulski)

Three photos of a damaged P-47D-30-RE s/n 44-20415 (A7-A) of 395th FS at Metz, France on 1 January 1945. Aircraft was damged on the ground during Operation Bodenplate.

(Kenneth Kik)

P-47D-40-RA

Following the introduction of the tear-drop hood and the cut-down rear fuselage, the Thunderbolt develope a problem: at high speeds the tail surfaces vibrated, and under extreme conditions the tail could detach. Th problem was eventually cured in a simple way: a dorsal fillet was added forward of the fin. The first versic to be factory-fitted with this was the D-40-RA. This batch was also fitted with the AN/APS-13 warning rad that informed the pilot of a threat behind. The K-14 gyro gun sight replaced the Mk VIII type used befor Under-wing attachments for Bazooka launchers were replaced with HVAR launchers (five under each wing).

All 665 aircraft of this batch were built at Farmingdale.

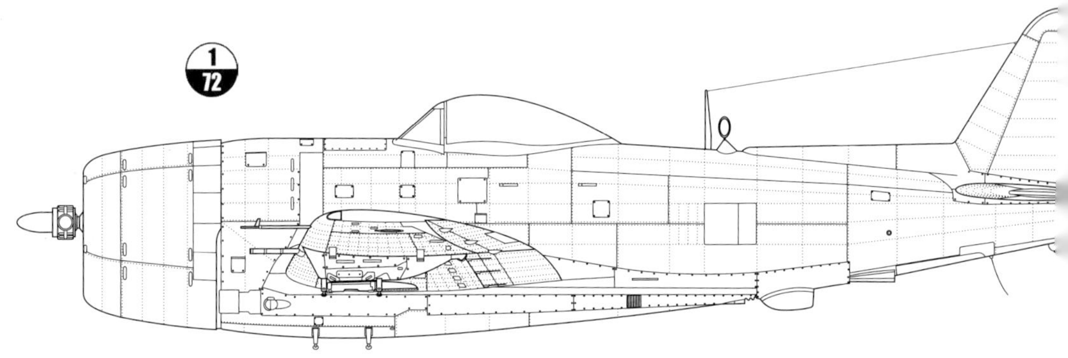

Scale plan of P-47D-40-RE.

P-47D-40-RA, (F-47D), s/n 45-49431 FE-481 of 7th FI Squadron, 1953.

(Stratus co.

YP-47M

Three P-47D-27-REs (nos. 42-27385, 42-27386 and 42-27388) were fitted with 2,800 hp R-2800-14W and then R-2800-57 engines with the new CH-5 supercharger. This even more powerful power plant was driving the new Curtiss Electric C642S-B40 propeller. Thanks to these modifications the Thunderbolt was able to reach a speed of 475 mph at an altitude of 32,000 ft.

P-47M-1-RE

Performance of the YP-47M was so promising that production of 130 aircraft designated P-47M-1-RE commenced at Farmingdale. The only unit to receive these machines was the 56th Fighter Group, 8th Air Force in Europe. Although initially delighted, pilots soon learned that the M variant suffered serious engine problems. Cooling was not adequate and the ignition system was prone to fail (especially at high altitudes). The R-2800-57 engine also proved very fuel-thirsty, which was a serious handicap for aircraft based in England and operating over Germany. Moreover, after a while the engines started to corrode, and had to be replaced. In order to retain the aeroplane in service it was necessary to introduce a number of modifications. The ignition system was improved, air flow through the engine bay was reduced, and the throttle was altered. A dorsal fillet was added on the rear fuselage, similar to that in the D-40. Some machines were even fitted with larger fillets, similar to those on the P-47N.

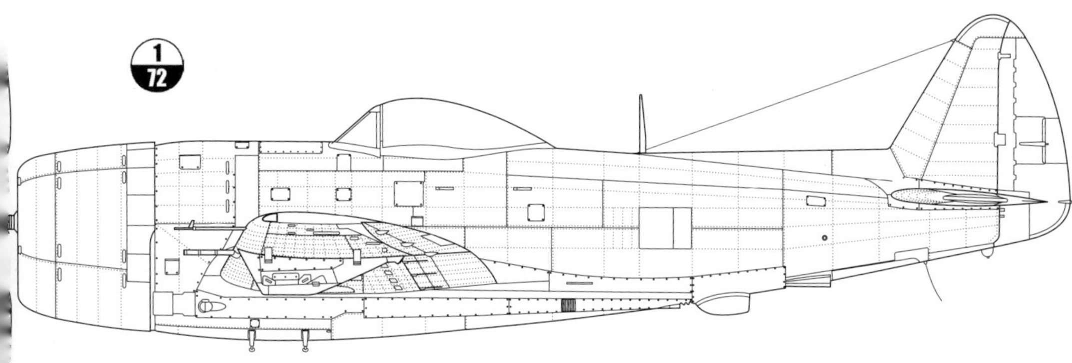

Above:
Scale plan of P-47M.

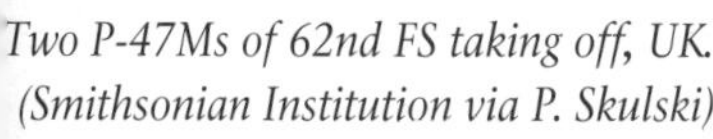

Two P-47Ms of 62nd FS taking off, UK.
(Smithsonian Institution via P. Skulski)

XP-47N

A new wing with tapered tip and span enlarged by 1 m, and with four internal fuel tanks, was first tested in the XP-47K. This was the prototype for a new version of the fighter, intended for long-range missions over Japan. In the summer of 1944 the P-47D-27-RE no. 42-27387 was fitted with new wings and the R-2800-57 engine (as used in the M). Air flow control flaps aft of the engine cowling were altered and modified with automatic control. Also the flow control flaps on the sides of the rear fuselage were modified in a similar way. The engine mount was redesigned, as was the electric generator. The undercarriage was changed and fitted with new, larger wheels. The internal fuel tankage was increased from 370 gallons (in the D) to 570 gallons.

To avoid any problems similar to those with the M variant, work on this version was carried out more slowly, and the aeroplane designated XP-47N was not ready until September 1944.

P-47N-1

Production P-47Ns were fitted with new dorsal fillets, larger than the D-40 ones, and with modified fuel and ignition systems. Initially the P-47N was intended for the 56th FG, but with the war in Europe over, they were sent to where they had initially been planned to operate, the Pacific theatre.

A total of 550 P-47N-1-REs were built at Farmingdale.

P-47N-5

The entire batch of 550 Thunderbolts of this version was completed at Farmingdale. The aircraft did not differ much externally from their predecessors. They were the first N variants with five HVAR launchers and the AN/APS-13 radar. Moreover, the Curtiss Electric C-1 automatic pilot and the homing radar were fitted. Last aircraft had R-2800-73 engines with electrically controlled ignition.

P-47N-5-RE, s/n 44-88512 at factory airfield. (Stratus coll.)

P-47N-1-RE, s/n 448819, '19', "Repulsive Thunderbox'. Unit unknown.

(Stratus coll.)

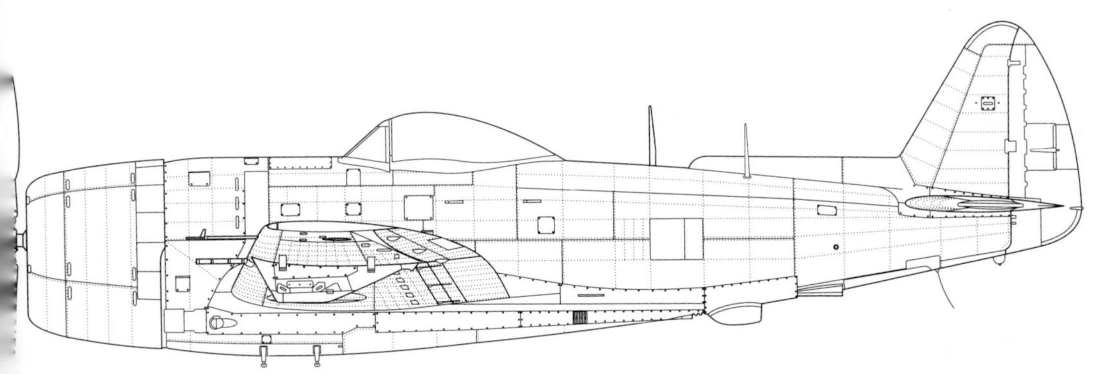

1/72

Scale plans of P-47N-5-RE.

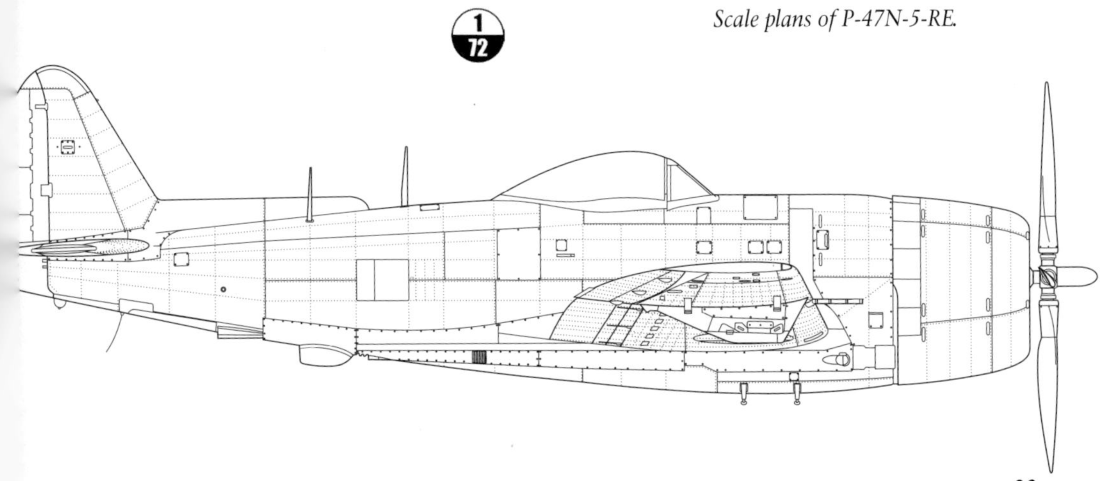

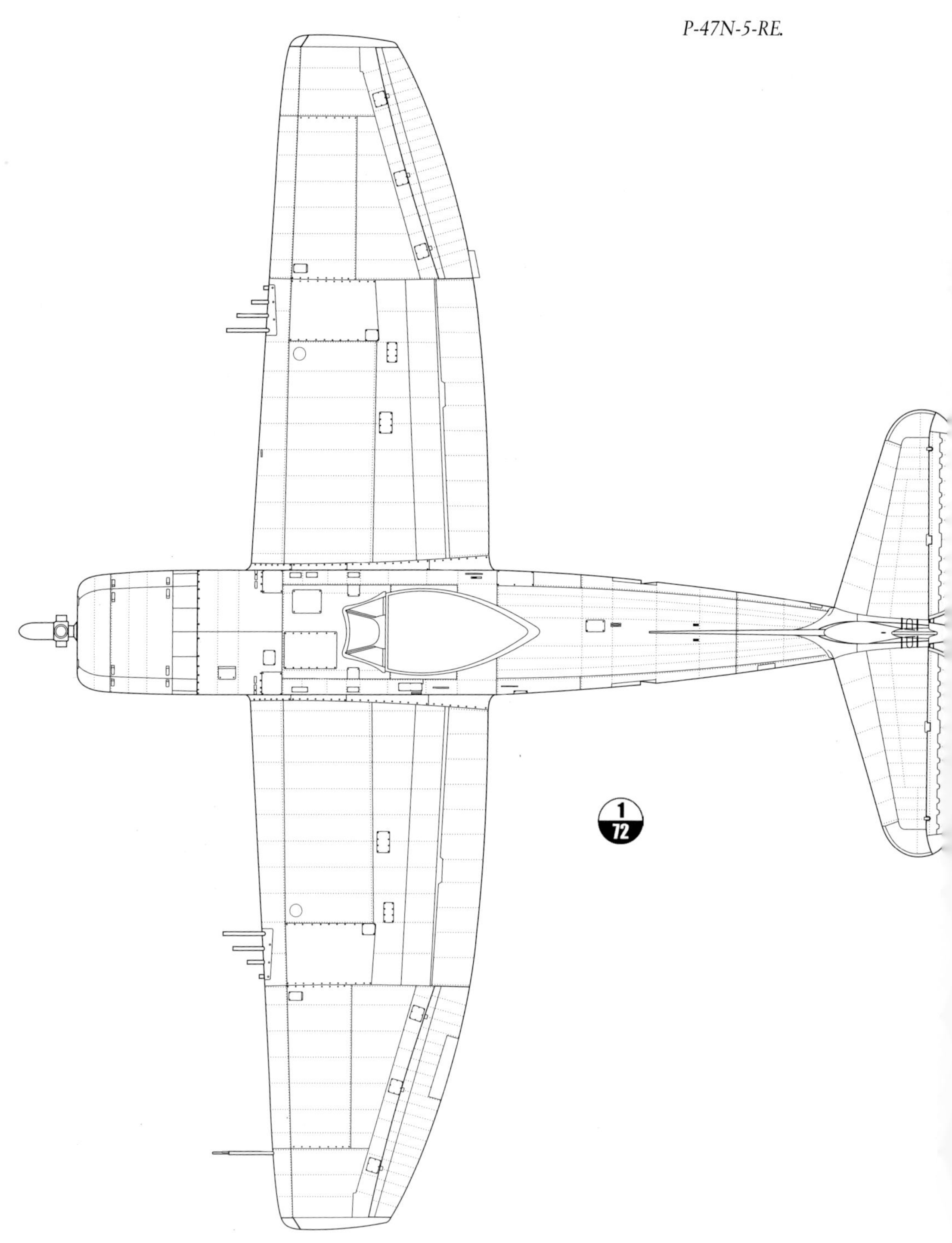
P-47N-5-RE.
1
72

P-47N-5-RE, serial 44-88680, PE-680, "Lois Mae" of 56th FS 61st FG, Selfridge Field (MI, USA).

(Stratus coll.)

Nice view of the P-47N wing platform.

(Stratus coll.)

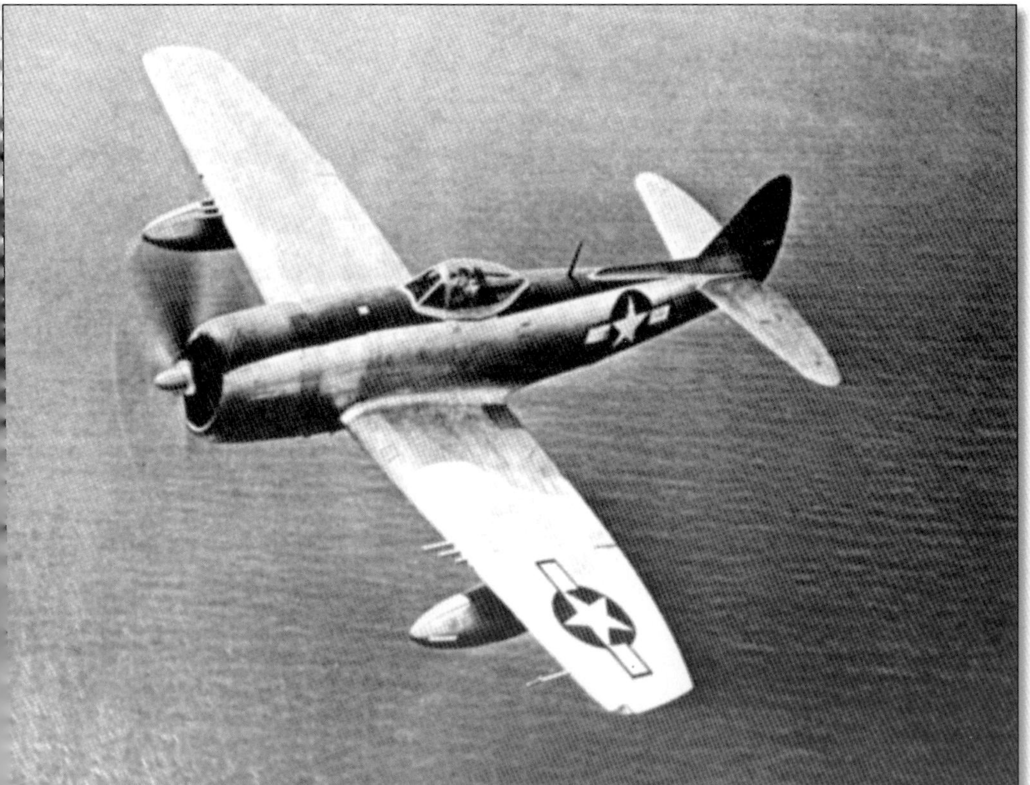

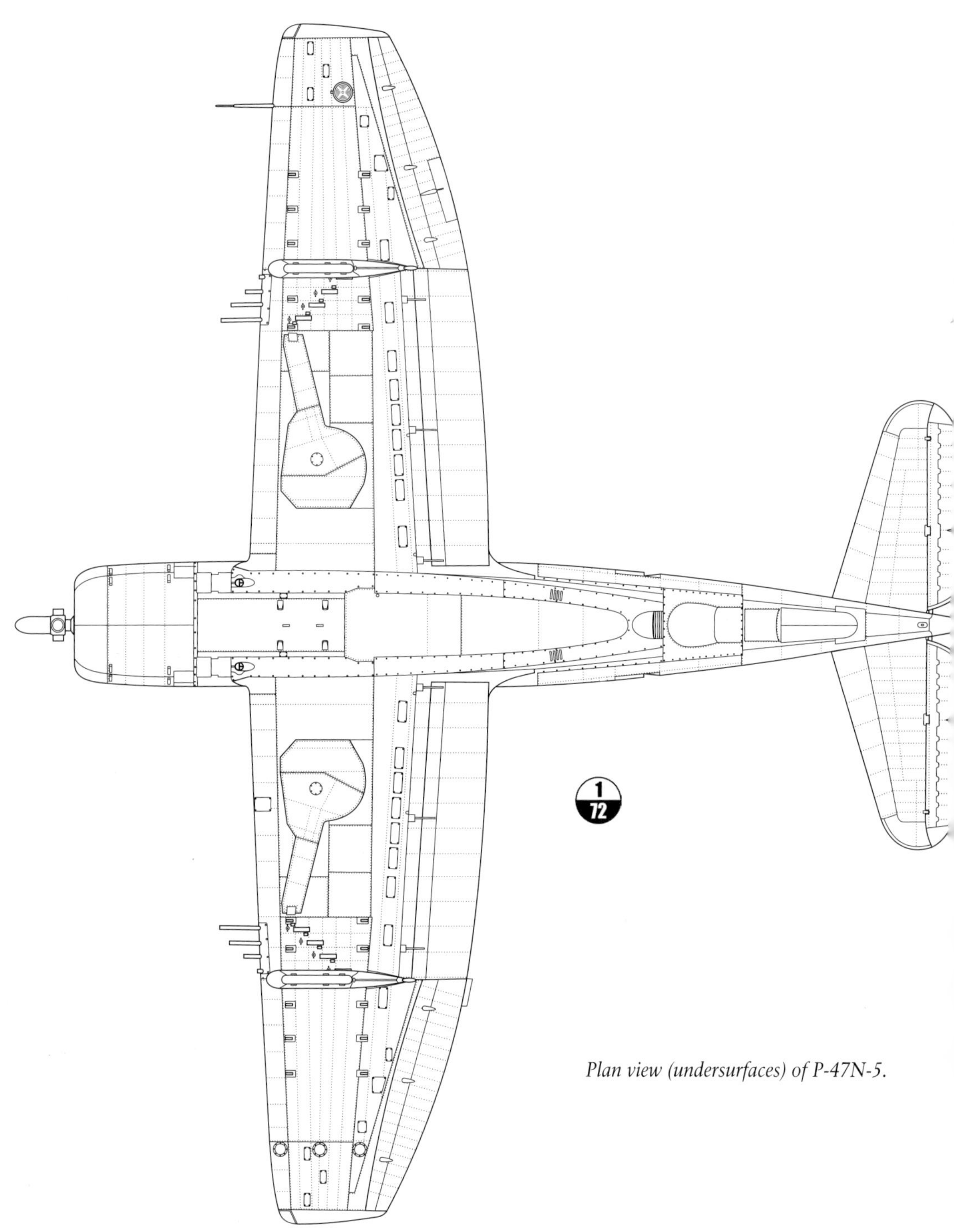

Plan view (undersurfaces) of P-47N-5.

P-47N-2

This was an in-field modification fitting of HVAR launchers on the P-47N-1. The N-1 aircraft fitted with the launchers were designated N-2.

P-47N-15

This version was powered by R-2800-73 engines. The machines were also fitted with a new pilot's seat type and K-14 gun sights (rather soon replaced with the more modern K-14A or K-14B). In place of the previous B-7 bomb carriers, new S-1 racks were introduced. All 200 P-47N-15s were built at Farmingdale.

P-47N-20-RE and RA

The N-20 batch featured a modified radio set and fuel system. A total of 349 aircraft of this version were built at Farmingdale and Evansville. Starting from the aeroplane no. 45-50051, new cockpit floor and rudder pedals started to be fitted at Evansville.

P-47N-25

These were the last production Thuderbolts. They were powered by a number of engine variants: R-2800-73, -77 and -81. From aeroplane no. 44-89294 on, the N-25 Thunderbolts were fitted with new cockpit floor and rudder pedals (similar to the N-20-RA). Flaps and ailerons were reinforced to withstand the rocket launch flame. All aircraft of this version were built at Farmingdale, and the last, 167th aeroplane was built after the war was over, in October 1945. Repositioning of the navigation lights from the leading edge to the middle of the wing tip was an externally noticeable modification.

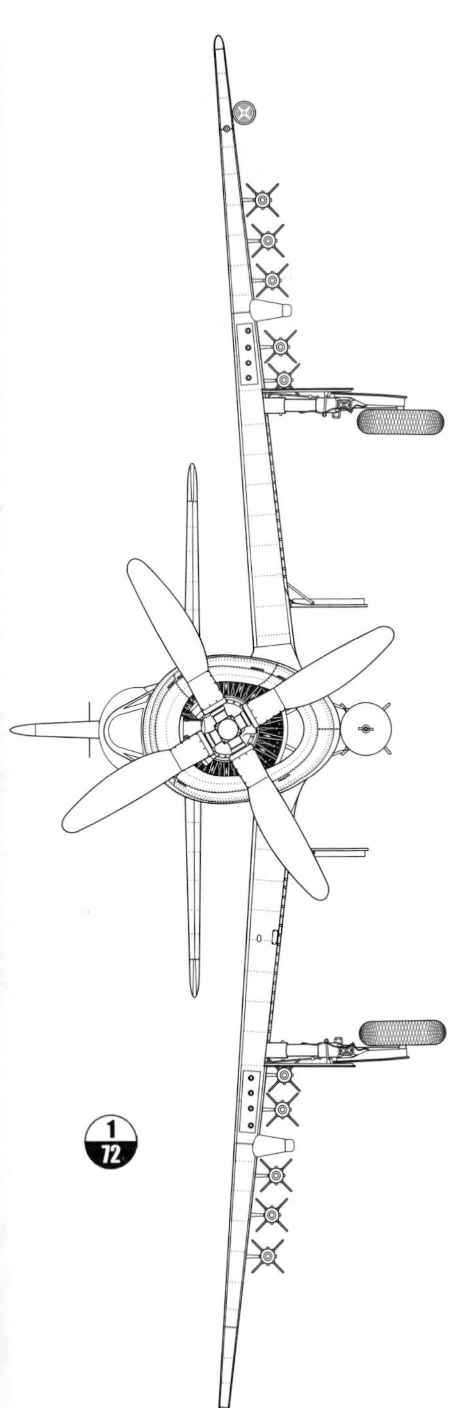

P-47N front view.

F-47D and N

In 1947 the US military aviation was reorganised, the USAAF becoming an independent service, the USA (United States Air Force). At the same time aircraft role designations were changed. Fighters were henceforwar identified by F for Fighter (rather than P for Pursuit). Numerous D and N Thunderbolts in Air National Guar units were subsequently redesignated the F-47.

P-47N-25 wings.

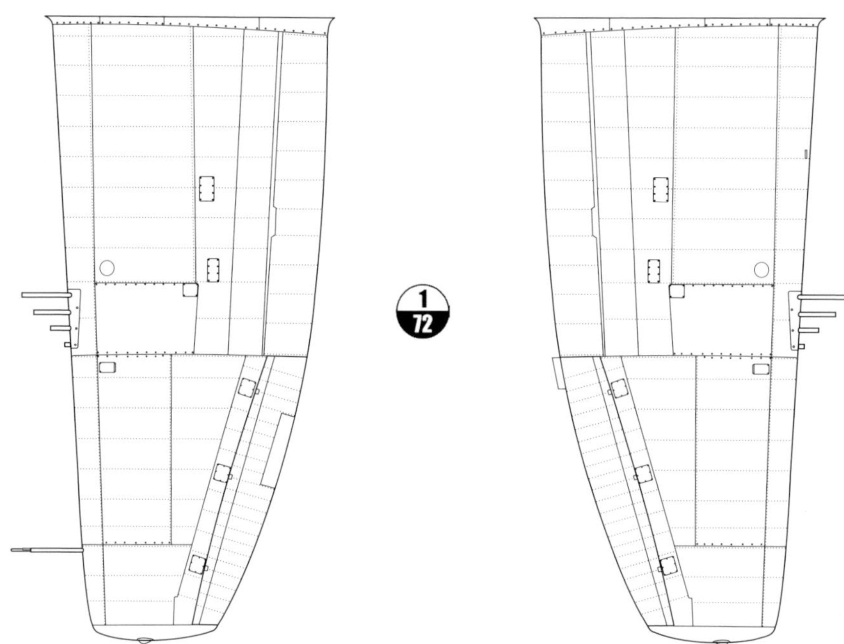

P-47N-20-RE, s/n 44-89116. Unit unknown.
(Stratus coll.)

P-47N-25 side view.

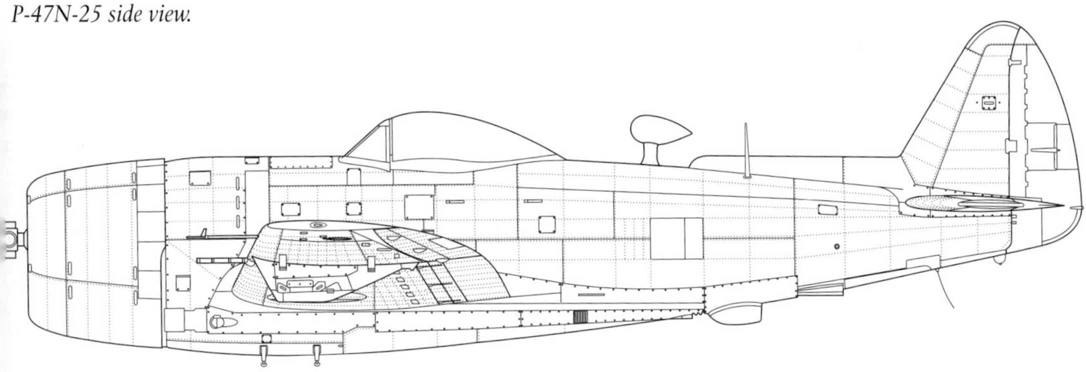

1/72

P-47N-25 fully armed.

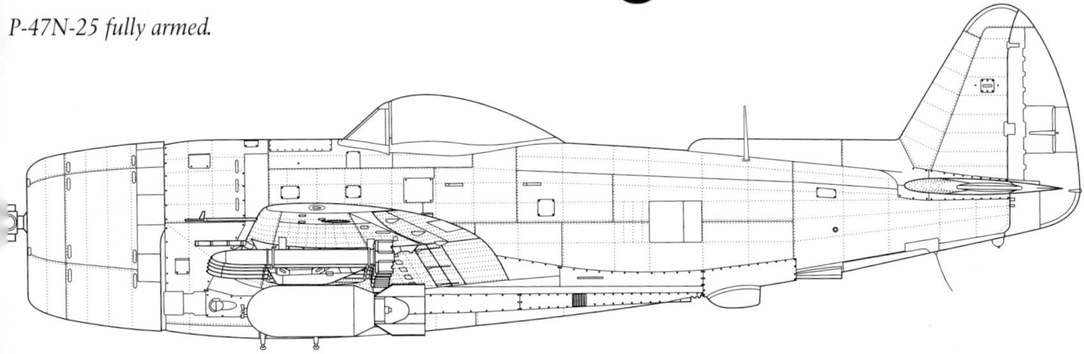

F-47N-20-RE, s/n/44-89140, FE-140-B of 332nd FG.
(US National Archives)

***Above** : P-47N-25-RE, s/n 44-89444 preserved at the Cradle of Aviation Museum, Garden City, New York, (USA) formerly of NG, 198th FS Puerto Rico Air National Guard - San Juan. Photo was taken in early 1970.*

(Stratus coll.)

***Below**: P-47N-25-RE, s/n 44-89425 preserved as agate guardian at Peterson Air and Space Museum, Colorado, USA. Aircraft was used by the Puerto Rico Air National Guard - San Juan (PR, USA).*

(MAP)

TECHNICAL DESCRIPTION

(P-47D-25~30 versions)

Republic P-47D Thunderbolt was a single-seat, single-engined fighter, cantilever low-wing monoplane with retractable undercarriage.

Wing: two-piece, straight, semi-elliptic with a bi-convex Kartveli/Republic S-3 aerofoil. Wing aspect ratio of 5.6, incidence 1°, dihedral (along upper surface) 4°. The structure was based on two steel main spars and two H-shaped auxiliary spars, plus 20 ribs in each half; skin of smooth duralumin sheets, riveted with conical rivets onto the spars, ribs, and L-shaped longerons. Ailerons and flaps attached to the rear auxiliary spar. Steel Friese-type ailerons were statically balanced: the port one was fitted with a trim tab, and the starboard one with a spring tab. Metal NACA slotted flaps were hydraulic actuated. Starting with the D-30 batch additional small split flaps were fitted on the forward auxiliary spar between the main wheel well and the gun compartment, to facilitate dive recovery. Wing tips were semi-circular.

Fuselage: duralumin monocoque design based on 20 frames connected by longerons. Forward of the fire-proof bulkhead, an eight-point tubular mount carried the engine covered with a NACA cowling featuring 8 hydraulic-operated exhaust flaps. 10 mm armour plates forward and aft of the cockpit.

Cockpit canopy: windscreen with built-in bullet-proof panel and a tear-drop shaped sliding hood.

Tail: conventional, cantilever, with the single fin and elevators of metal construction, duralumin-covered, completed as one section and bolted onto the rear fuselage.

Tail control surfaces: duralumin-covered, fitted with 3 trim tabs. Fin offset 1° to port to compensate for the propeller torque.

Undercarriage: main wheels with single oleo legs, attached to the forward auxiliary spar, retracted hydraulically inwards into the wings. To provide proper propeller clearance, when lowered the legs were extended by 0.23 m, due to the substantial propeller diameter and the limited undercarriage bay volume. Tail wheel with shock-absorber, coupled with the rudder, fully retractable backwards into the fuselage.

Two photos of the engine of P-47D-28-RE "Lady Grace" of 395th FS, 368th FG, 9th AF. Personal aircraft of Larry Marsch.

(Kenneth Kik)

Power plant: Pratt & Whitney R-2800 Double Wasp turbo-supercharged, 18-cylinder, air cooled, four-stroke, double row radial, used in several sub-variants, as described in the text above. Cubic capacity of all variants: 45,945 cc, cylinder bore 146.04 mm, stroke 152.39 mm, outside diameter of the engine 1,325 mm, weight 1,005-1,045 kg

Propeller: all-metal, constant speed, four-bladed (see description of individual aircraft versions).

Turbo-supercharger system: exhaust piping for the turbine drive went along the sides of the bottom fuselage, the excess gases spilling immediately aft of the engine, via two openings near the wing leading edge. The main exhaust outlet was located forward of the tail wheel.

Carburettor air intake was located under the engine, between the intakes of two oil coolers. The air was fed through a large duct in the very bottom of the fuselage. Aft of the cockpit the duct was split in three: the central one fed the air to the supercharger, and the other two to the air coolers, from which it was let out via openings in the sides of the fuselage. Upon leaving the supercharger the carburettor air was cooled in the air coolers in the rear fuselage and then fed through two ducts along fuselage sides, above the wing. The whole system provided boost pressures of 1,770 hPa at an altitude of 10,700 m, and a ceiling of 12-13,000 m.

Drop tanks.

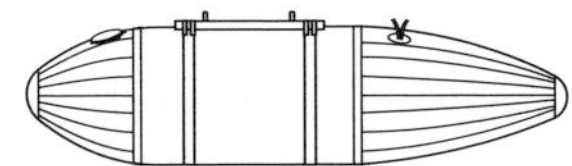

150 gal, 570 l, paper.

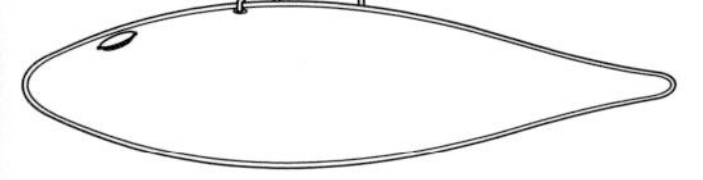

165 gal, 625 l.

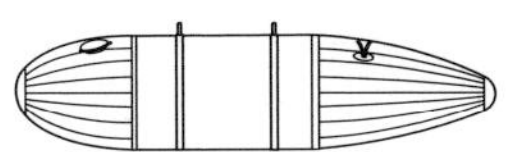

108 gal, 410 l, paper.

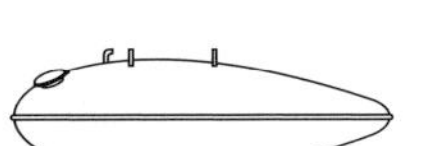

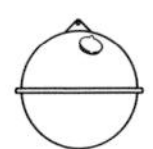

75 gal, 283 l.

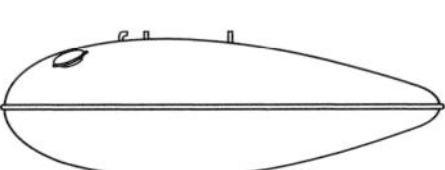

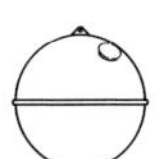

110 gal, 415 l.

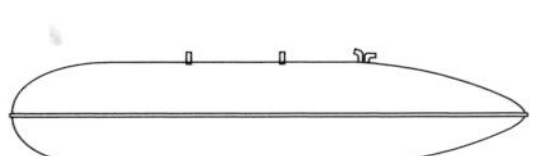

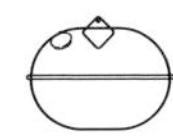

200 gal, 760 l.

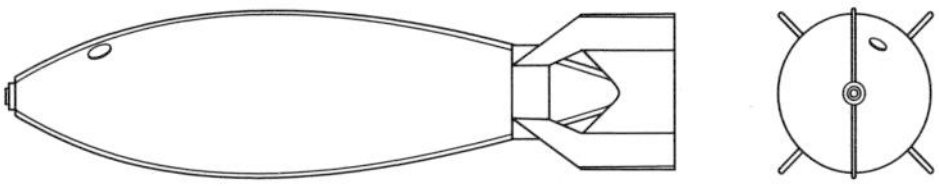

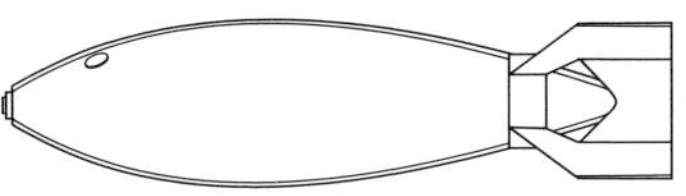

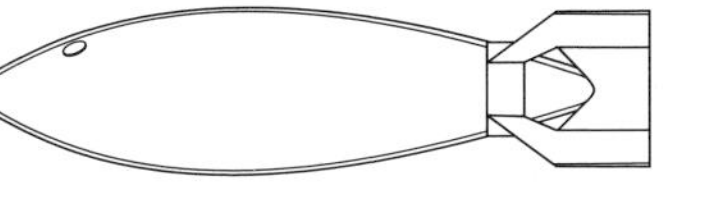

165 gal, 625 l, water bomb.

Ammunition loading before the next mission. Saipan, 7th AF, 1944.

(US National Archives)

Oil system: 108 l tank forward of the fire-proof bulkhead; two oil coolers below the engine, with adjustable outlets forward of the wing leading edge.

Fuel system: two armoured, self-sealing tanks in the fuselage: the main 1,020 l tank forward of the cockpit, and the auxiliary 380 l tank immediately aft of it, under the cockpit.

The following external tanks were used:

— 75 US gall. (285 l), tear-drop shaped, metal, US production (as in the P-39, P-40, and P-51);

— 110 US gall. (415 l), tear-drop shaped, metal, US production (as in the P-51);

— 108 US gall (410 l), cigar-shaped, paper, British production (as in the Hurricane);

— 150 US gall. (570 l), cigar-shaped, paper, British production

— 200 US gall. (760 l), flat, metal, US production.

— 165 US gall. (625 l) under-wing tanks, tear-drop shaped, metal, US production (as in the P-38).

Maximum permissible tank drop speed — 370 km/h.

115 l tank for water/methanol short-time engine rating increase mixture was used.

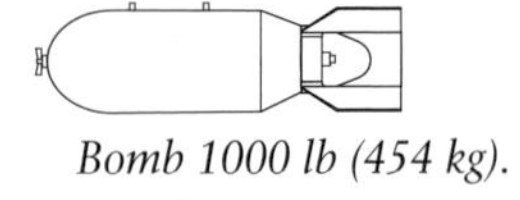

Bomb 1000 lb (454 kg).

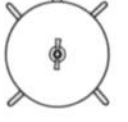

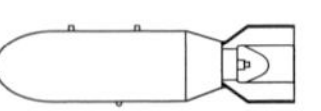

Bomb 500 lb (227 kg).

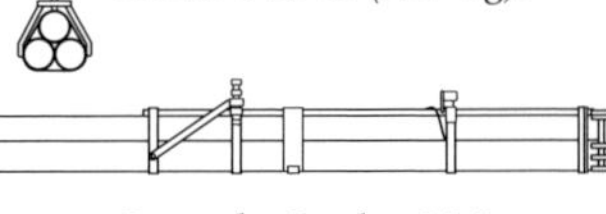

Bazooka Rocket M-8.

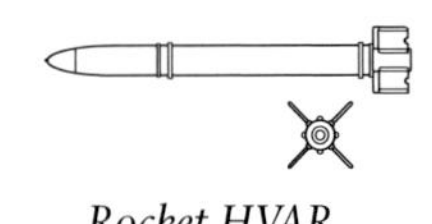

Rocket HVAR.

Electric system*:* generator and 24 V battery forward of the bullet-proof bulkhead, under the oil tank; landing light in the starboard wing, single navigation lights in wing tips, rear light in the rudder, formation light on top of the fuselage aft of the cockpit. Three recognition lights in the starboard wing at the tip (red, blue and yellow).

Other systems: oxygen system fed by six cylinders located aft of the pilot's seat; SCR-774 VHF radio set, N-9 reflector gun sight or (from the P-47D-35 on) K-14 gyro gun sight.

Armament: eight wing-mounted 0.5 in. Browning M-2 machine guns, firing outside the propeller disc. Guns harmonised at 135 to 275 m, depending on the pilot's preference. Ammunition belts, 425 rounds per gun, housed between the first and second spars, outboard of the main wheel wells.

Bomb carriers: under the fuselage and under wings.

Bomb load: 500 or 1,000 lb. (227 or 454 kg), the latter under wings only.

Starting from the P-47D-35 batch, zero-length launchers for 5 in. rockets; provision to take 10 rockets with the under-wing bomb/tank carriers empty, or 6 rockets with wing stores. All versions could carry triple 114 mm Bazooka M-8 launchers under both wings, underneath the guns, with the ammunition capacity reduced to 4x267 rounds per wing. These were not normally used after the introduction of the HVAR missiles.

Camera gun in the starboard wing root.

Opposite page: *P-47D inthe CBI Theatre.*
(US National Archives)

P-47 Thunderbolt 'Bubbletop' specification

Version		P-47D-28-RE	P-47M-1	P-47N-1
Engine		R-2800-59	R-2800-57, "C- series"	R-2800-57, "C- series"
Power max./boost	[hp]	2,000/2,300	2,100/2,800	2,100/2,800
Wing span	[ft] [m]	40 ft 9.25" 12.42	40 ft 9.25" 12.42	42 ft 6.8" 12.97
Wing area	[sq ft]	300	300	322
Length	[ft] [m]	36 ft 1.75" 11.02	36 ft 1.75" 11.02	36 ft 1.75" 11.02
Heigth [m]	[ft] [m]	14 ft 8"	14 ft 8"	14 ft 6" 4.47
Weight empty	[lb] [kg]	10,000 4,500	10,340 4,700	10,988 4,984
gross	[lb] [kg]	14,500 6,600	15,340 6,800	13,823 6,270
max take-off	[lb] [kg]	17,500 7,900	18,250 8,200	21,200 9,600
Top speed	[mph] [km/h]	428 690	475 761	467 752
at	[ft] [m]	30,000 9,100	32,000 9,750	32,000 9,750
Landing speed	[mph] [km/h]	171	158	158
Rate of climb	[min to altitude]	6.2 min to 15,000 ft 6.2/4,500	13.5 min to 32,000 ft 5/4,600	14.2 min to 25,000 ft 9/4,600
Service ceiling	[ft] [m]	42,000 12,800	41,000 12,500	40,000 13,100
Max range	[miles] [km]	1,030 at 10,000 ft 1600	530 (normal) 850	2,200

Production runs of the P-47 'Bubbletop'

Version	Quantity	Serial numbers	Engine	Propeller	Dorsal fin
P-47D-25-RE	385	42-26389 to 42-26773	R-2800-59	HS	
P-47D-26-RA	250	42-28189 to 42-28438	R-2800-59	A	
P-47D-27-RE	611	42-26774 to 42-27384	R-2800-59	HS	
P-47D-28-RA	1028	42-28439 to 42-29466	R-2800-59	A	
P-47D-28-RE	750	44-19558 to 44-20307	R-2800-59	A	
P-47D-30-RE	800	44-20308 to 44-21107	R-2800-59	A	small (retrofitted)
P-47D-30-RA	1800	44-32668 to 44-33867 44-89684 to 44-90283	R-2800-59	B	
P-47D-40-RA	665	44-90284 to 44-90483 45-49090 to 45-49554	R-2800-59	B	small
P-47M-1-RE	130	44-21108 to 44-21237	R-2800-57	B40	small, fitted after production
P-47N-1-RE	550	44-87784 to 44-88333	R-2800-57	B40	large
P-47N-5-RE	550	44-88334 to 44-88883	R-2800-57, -73	B40	large
P-47N-15-RE	200	44-88884 to 44-89083	R-2800-73	B40	large
P-47N-20-RE	200	44-89084 to 44-89283	R-2800-73, -77	B40	large
P-47N-20-RA	149	45-49975 to 45-50123	R-2800-73, -77	B40	large
P-47N-25-RE	167	44-89284 to 44-89450	R-2800-73, -77, -81	B40	large

Propellers:
HS – Hamilton Standard Hydromatic 24E50, dia 13' 1 7/8"
A – Curtiss-Electric C542S-A114, dia 13'
B – Curtiss-Electric C642S-B, dia 13'
B40 – Curtiss-Electric C642S-B40, dia 13'

P-47D-30 of Ecuador AF.
(J. Delgado)

Thunderbolt II

Britain ordered a total of 918 Thunderbolts, allocated to squadrons operating in Burma. The first 240 were in the P-47D-22-RE ('razorback') version, the remainder featuring tear-drop shaped hoods. The latter were designated the Thunderbolt II (see table below). The last 88 machines were never delivered, as the order was cancelled at the end of the war.

P-47D-25-RE	HD182-HD271	90
P-47D-27-RE	HD272-HD301	30
P-47D-28-RE	KJ128-KJ297	170
P-47D-30-RE	KJ298-KJ367 KL168-KL347	250
P-47D-30-RA	KL838-KL886	49
P-47D-40-RA	KL887	1

Thunderbolt II of No 258 Squadron RAF, Ratnap, Burma, 1945.

(Stratus coll.)

***Below:** P-47D-28-RE s/n 44-19631, Thunderbolt II, KJ140 of 30 Squadron in India and Burma. This plane was damaged during a storm at Chakulia, India on 23 May 1945.*

(Stratus coll.)

Other Foreigner Users

Country	Quantity	Years in use
France	446	1944-1960
USSR	196	1944-1947
Brazil	136	1944-1947
Taiwan	240	1947-1961
Turkey	235	1948-1954
Iran	150	1948-1959
Italy	75	1945-1950
Chile	48	1948-1960
Yugoslavia	150	1951-1959
Portugal	50	1952-1956
Mexico	25	1944-1962
Columbia	35	1947-1958
Bolivia	20	1947-1965
Ecuador	20	1947-1966
Peru	20	1947-1964
Venezuela	20	1947-1964
Nicaragua	25	1947-1964
Dominica	25	1948-1964
Honduras	20	1951-1966

P-47D-25 of the Italian Air Force, 1948.

(Stratus coll.)

Above: *P-47D of the Mexican Air Force's 201 Squadron, which was attached to the AAF's 58th FG.*

Below: *P-47D-28-RA, s/n 42-29088 (foreground) and P-47D-30-RA, s/n 44-33710 of 201 Sqn, 58th FG.*
Both photos (US National Archives)

Bibliography

Books

Angelucci Enzo, Bowers, Peter; *The American Fighter*, Orion Books, 1987
Bell, Dana; *Air Forces Colors Vol. 2*, Squadron/Signal Publications, Carrollton, 1997
Bell, Dana; *Air Forces Colors Vol. 3*, Squadron/Signal Publications, Carrollton, 1997
Davies, Larry; *P-47 Thunderbolt in Action No 67*, Squadron/Signal Publications, Carrollton, 1984
Drendel, Lou; *P-47 Tbunderbolt, Walk Around Number 11*, Squadron/Signal Publications, Carrollton, 1997
Freeman, Roger; Thunderbolt: *A Documentary History of the Republic P-47*, Motorbooks, 1992
Freeman, Roger; *American Eagles, P-47 Thunderbolt Units of the Eight Air Force*, Classic Publications, 2002
Hall, Alan; *Warpaint Special No.1 "Republic P-47 Thunderbolt"*, Warpaint
Jarski, A. Michulec; R.; *P-47 Thunderbolt, ML 25 & ML 26*, AJ-Press, Gdynia 1996
Johnsen, F.A.; *Republic P-47 Thunderbolt*, WarbirdTech Series Vol. 23, Speciality Press, 1999
Johnson, Robert S. Caidin, Martin; *Thunderbolt!*, Ballantine Books, 1958
Kinzey, Bert; P-47 Thunderbolt, *D&S vol. 54*, Squadron/Signal Publications, Carrollton, 1998
Mietelski, Michał; *Samolot myśliwski P-47 Thunderbolt*, TBiU 158, Bellona, Warszawa 1994
Nohara, S. Okazaki; N.; *Republic P-47 Thunderbol*t, AeroDetal 14 Dai Nippon Kaiga Co, 1995
Przemysław, Skulski; *P-47 Thunderbolt, Bubbletop*, ACE Publications, 1998
Rabbets, J. B.; *Republic P-47D Thunderbolt*, AeroData International No 6, Vintage Aviation Publications, 1978
Scutts, Jerry; *Republic P-47 Thunderbolt*, Combat Legend Airlife Publishing, 2004
Scutts, Jerry; *Republic P-47 Thunderbolt*, The Operational Record Motorbooks International, 1998
Shacklady, Edward; *The Republic P-47D Thunderbolt*, Aircraft in Profile, Doubleday, 1969
Swanborough, Gordon, Bowers, Peter M.; *United States Military Aircraft since 1909*, Smithsonian, 1989
Wagner, Ray; *American Combat Planes*, Third Enlarged Edition, Doubleday, 1982
Wiśniewski, Piotr; *Republic P-47D Bubbletop MDPM No 15*, Rossagraph, 2002

P-47D, A7-Q of 395th FS, 368th FG flown by Charlie Rife taxiing at Metz. (Kenneth Kik)

GENERAL VIEW

Above: *Thunderbolt II, P-47D-40-RA, serial 45-49295, delivered to the RAF. Painted as a machine of 30 Squadron SEAC, RS-L, UK serial KL216. Aircraft preserved in Cosford Aerospace Museum, UK.*

(R. Pęczkowski)

Below: *P-47D-40-RA, serial 44-90368, painted as aircraft of 366th FS, 358th FG. Airworthy a/c at Lone Star Flight Museum, Galveston, Texas, USA.*

(P. Wiśniewski)

Above: P-47Ds of 368th FG, 397th FS during overhaul in hanger at Straubing AB, Germany, 1945.

(Kenneth Kik)

***Below**: P-47D-30-RE, s/n 44-20355 of GC II/5 French Air Force.*

(via P. Skulski)

Above: P-47D-40-RA, s/n 45-59458, restored as "44-20344", "Norma" of 65th FS, 57th FG. New England Air Museum, Windsor Locks, Connecticut.

(P. Wiśniewski)

***Below:** P-47D-30-RA, French Air Force preserved at* Musee de l'Air *at Le Bourget.*

(J. Kightly)

Top: *P-47D-40 painted as "Oregons Britania", composite static restoration, personal aircraft of Hubert "Hub" Zemke, CO 56th FG, at Duxford, UK.*

(J. Kightly)

Above: *P-47D, a composite machine from parts of D and N versions. Painted as 42-26671, of 83th FS, 78th FG.*

(via P. Skulski)

Below: *P-47D-30-RA of Yugoslav Air Force.*

(G. Papadimitriou via P. Skulski)

Above:
P-47D, a composite machine from parts of D and N versions. Painted as 42-26671, of 83th FS.
(via P. Skulski)

Left:
Two photos of Turkish F-47D-30-RA preserved at Turkish Air Force Museum, Istanbul.
(G. Papadimitriou via P. Skulski)

Above: *Rear view of P-47D, Duxford, UK.* *(R. Pęczkowski)*
Right: *Portside of P-47D preserved at museum in Beijing, China.* *(M. Orlog)*
Below: *P-47D, "Snortin' Bull 3rd". of 404th FG. Personal aircraft of James Mullins.* *(via P. Skulski)*

FUSELAGE

Right: *Port, center, part of P-47D fuselage.*
(P. Wiśniewski)

Right: *Access panel below cockpit.*

Below: *Starboard side of the fuselage. The big square access panel is for the oxygen tanks, and the access panel to the filler cap (red square) of the 100-gallon fuel tank under the pilot's seat.*

Below, right: *Port, rear part of the fuselage. The intercooler exhaust doors in open position are visible.*
(All photos P. Wiśniewski)

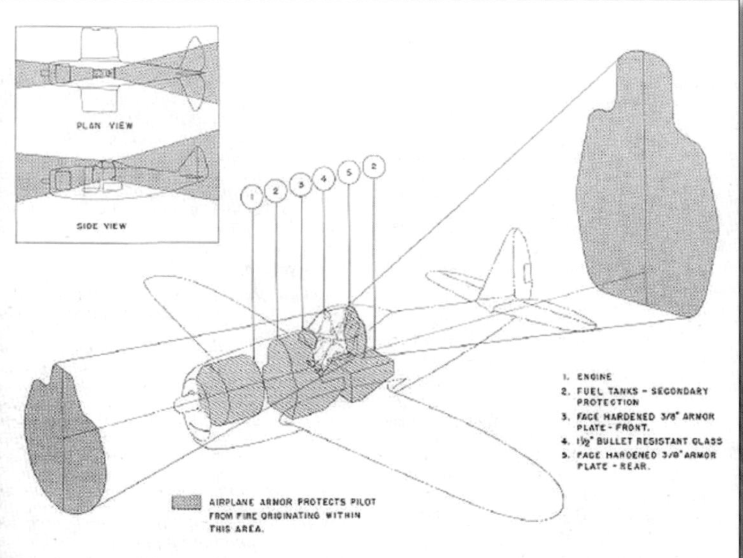

P-47D pilot protection. (Drawing from the Pilot's Manual)

Two photos of the intercooler exhaust doors. The first shows the doors in fully open position and the last in the fully closed position. The doors slide and open.

(P. Wiśniewski)
(G. Papadimitriou via P. Skulski)

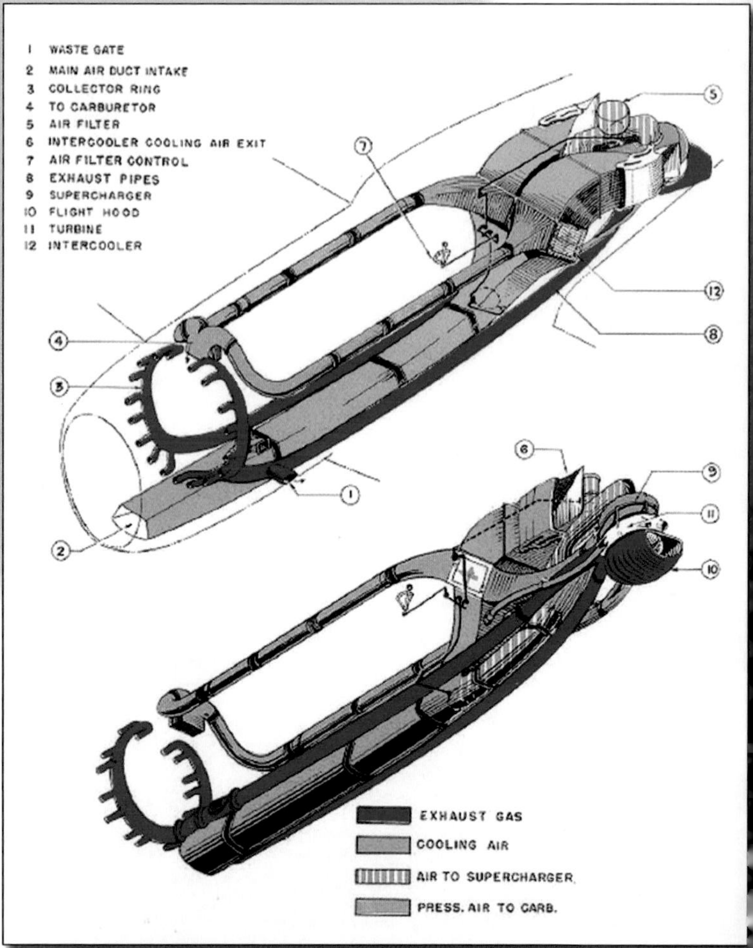

P-47D exhaust and supercharger system.
(Drawing from Pilot's manual)

1 WASTE GATE
2 MAIN AIR DUCT INTAKE
3 COLLECTOR RING
4 TO CARBURETOR
5 AIR FILTER
6 INTERCOOLER COOLING AIR EXIT
7 AIR FILTER CONTROL
8 EXHAUST PIPES
9 SUPERCHARGER
10 FLIGHT HOOD
11 TURBINE
12 INTERCOOLER

EXHAUST GAS
COOLING AIR
AIR TO SUPERCHARGER
PRESS. AIR TO CARB.

Supercharger exchange in the field.
(US National Archive)

Two photos of the central fuselage cooling louvers. In the middle photo the drain cocks, located just aft of the right wing root, are also visible.
(P. Wiśniewski)

Port side of the central fuselage. Note the different shades of the panels. The red line is the handgrip. Above the grip is access panel to the 1.5 gallon supercharger oil tank.
(R. Pęczkowski)

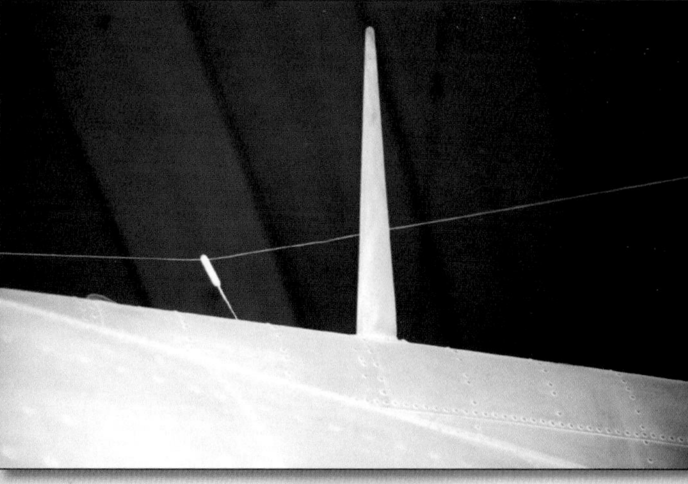

***Top photos and right photo**: Antenna mast and aerial mounting at the fuselage. Note the offset to the right of the antenna wire mounting.*

(P. Wiśniewski)

Above left:
Port side, front part of the P-47D fuselage.

(R. Pęczkowski)

Left:
Port side central part of the fuselage, just below the cockpit.

(via P. Skulski)

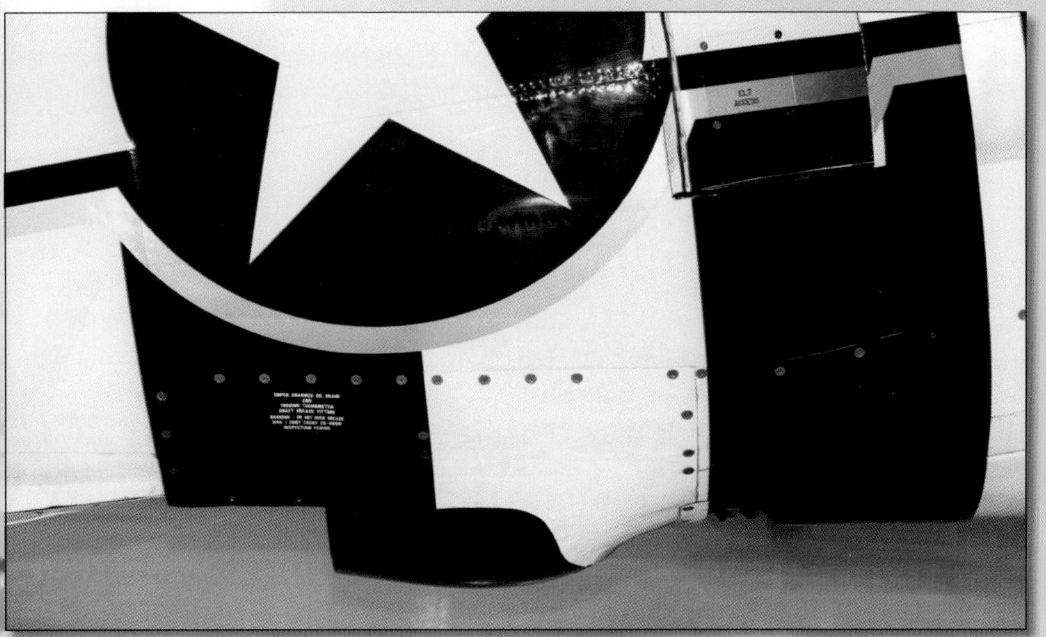

Turbocharger exhaust fairing (shroud) beneath the fuselage.

(P. Wiśniewski)

(via P. Skulski)

Top photo: *Upper part of the fuselage, just in front of the canopy.*

Above left: *This is P-47D, FAB419662 (D5). It was flown by the 2nd Lieutenant Alberto Martins Torres, and took part of 99 missions in Italy during WWII. The 1° Grupo de Aviaçao de Caça - 1° GAVCA (1st Brazilian Fighter Squadron) badge is clearly seen.*

(Guilherme Furtado Filho)

Above, right and below: *Two photos of the rear fuselage access panel.*

(P. Wiśniewski)

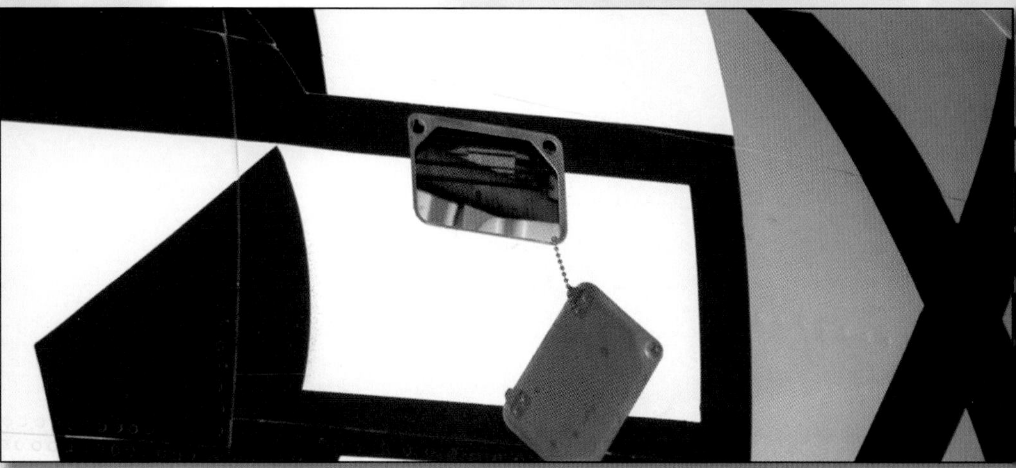

Left:
Starboard side of the front fuselage.
(P. Wiśniewski)

Below:
Two photos of the 110 gallon fuel tank under the fuselage.
(P. Wiśniewski)

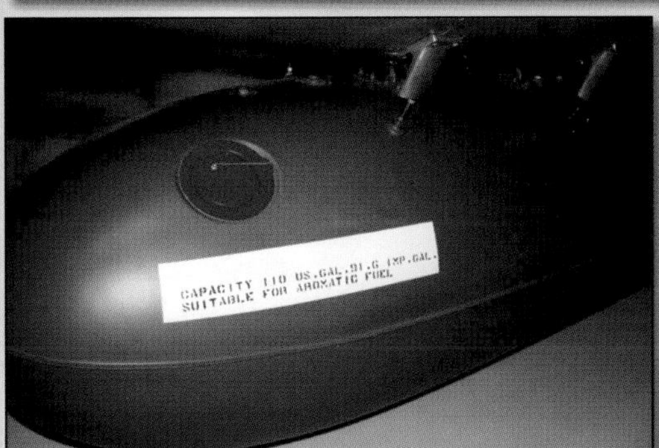

Bottom of the page:
Fuselage of the P47D-40-RA, serial 45-49346 under restoration.
(M. Orlog)

WING

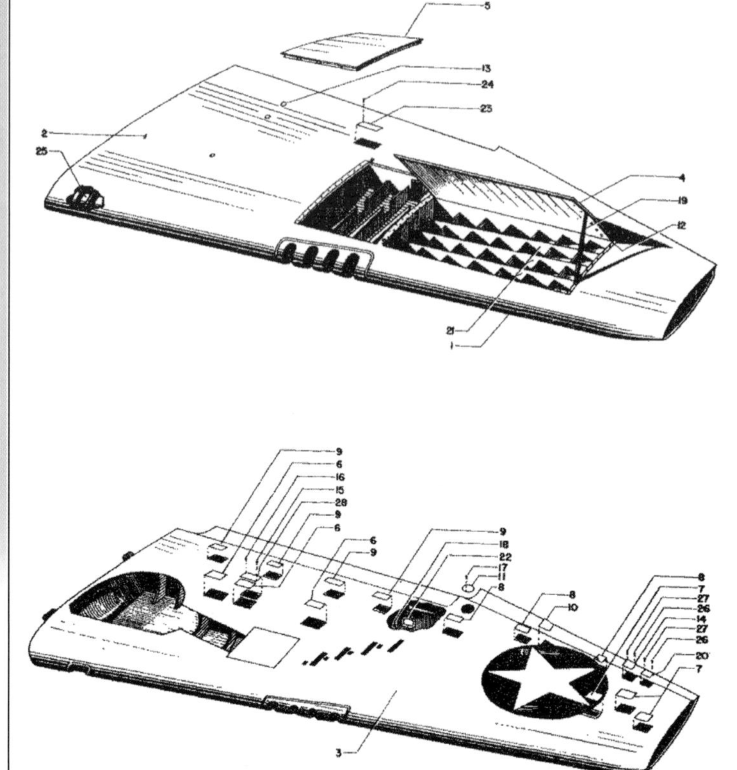

Wing removeable panels. (Drawings from P-47 Maintenance Instruction)

Below:
Starboard wing of the P-47 preserved in Technical Museum Zagreb, Croatia.

(M. Orlog)

Port wing of the P-47.
(P. Przymusiała)

Uppersurface of the landing flap in down position, starboard wing.
(P. Wiśniewski)

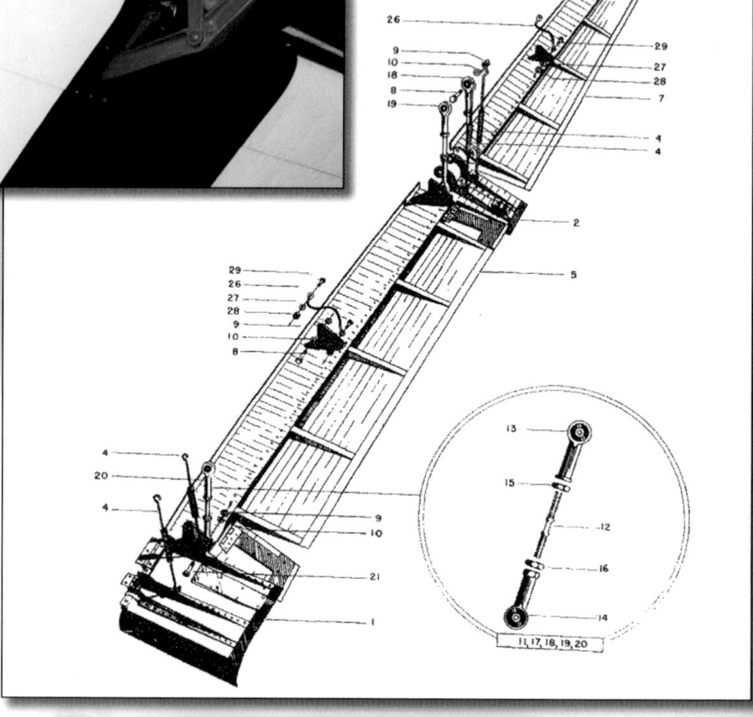

Landing flaps construction.
(Drawing from P-47 Maintenance Instruction)

Two photos of the undersurface of the landing flap. The large flap hinges are visible.
Photos. (P. Wiśniewski)

Above and left: *Two close up photos of landing flap hinges.*

(P. Wiśniewski)

Reinforced step area on the wing fillet

(P. Przymusiała)

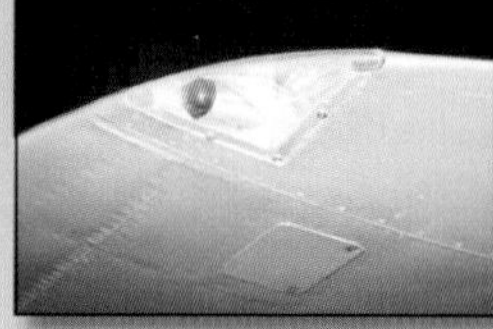

Above:
Port wingtip, red navigation lamp is visible.
(R. Pęczkowski)

Right:
Starboard aileron, fixed trim tab is visible.
(via P. Skulski)

Right and above, right:
Two photos of the wingtips. Three identification lights are visible. They were red, green and amber, from front to rear.
(P. Wiśniewski)

Above and left: *Two photos of aileron hinges with their fairing.*
Left: *Close up photo of the identification lights.*
Below: *Photo of the wing uppersurfaces.*
Below, left: *Two photos of the underwing compressibility flaps in open position.*

(All photos P. Wiśniewski)

Above and right: *Two photos of the pitot tube on the leading edge of the port wing. Note the landing light under the port wing.*

(P. Wiśniewski)

Below: *Photos of the cockpit cooling air inlet and gun camera with its small rectangular lens.*

(R. Pęczkowski)

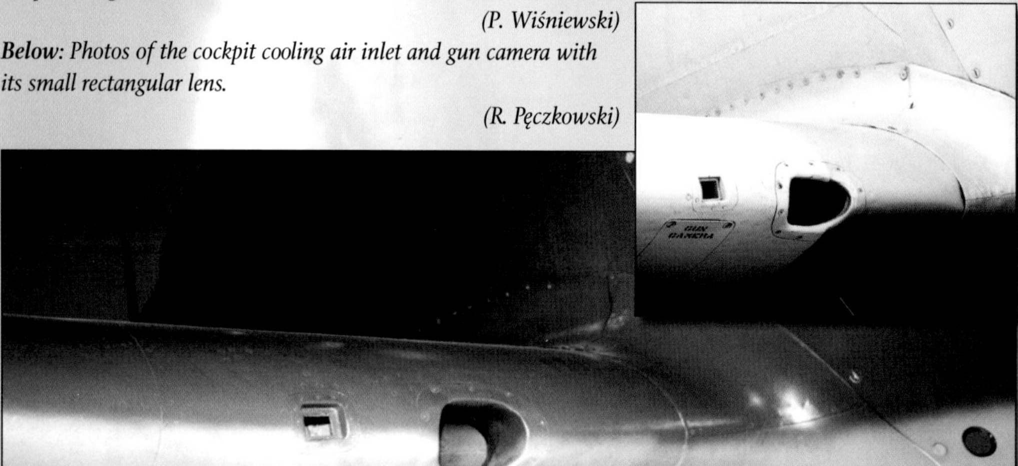

CANOPY

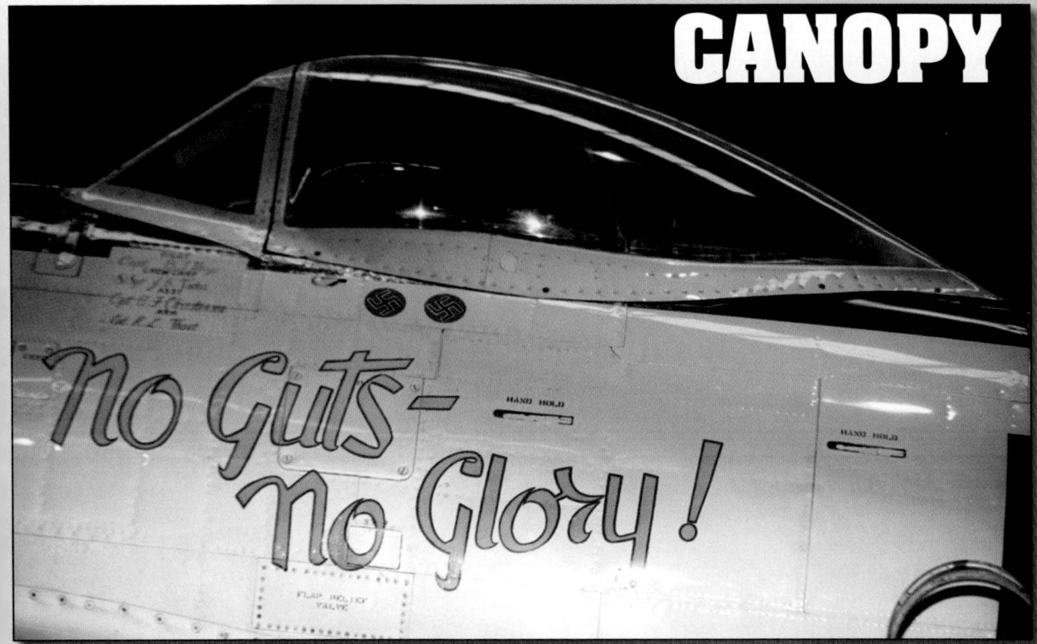
No Guts-
No Glory!
HAND HOLD
HAND HOLD
FLAP RELIEF VALVE

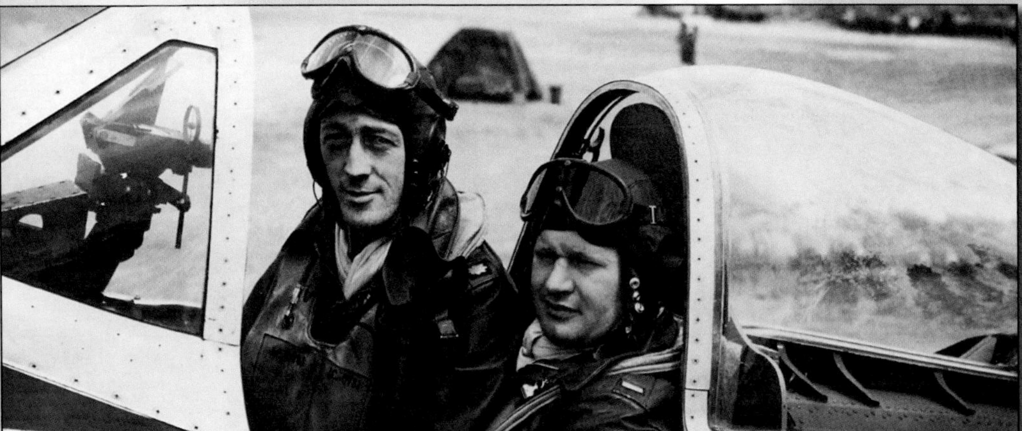
HAND HOLD

This and previous page, top: *Canopy in closed position.*
(P. Wisniewski)

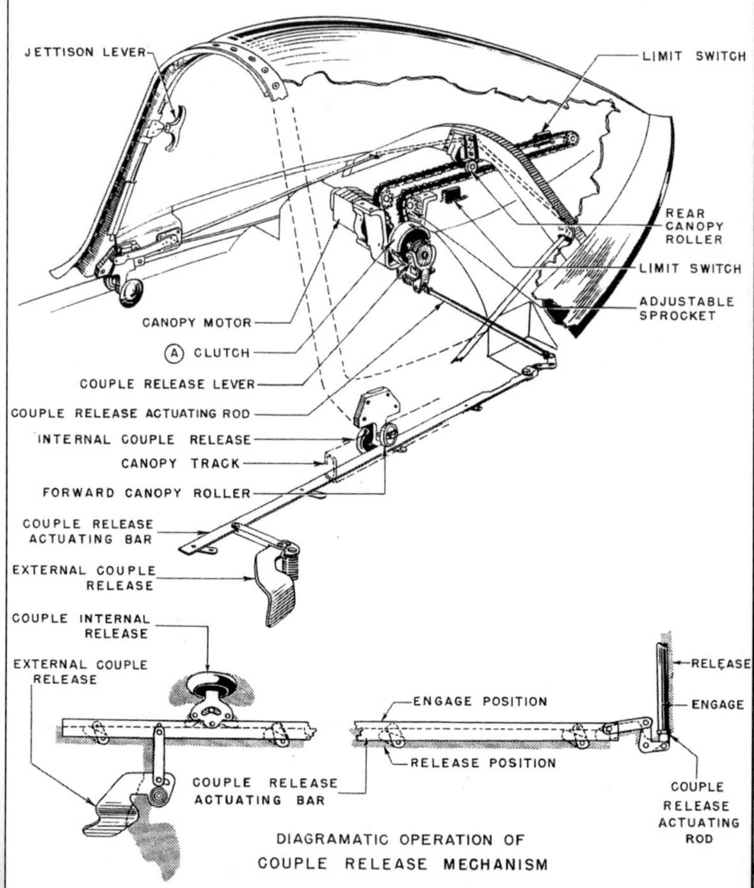

Canopy operating mechanism.
(Drawing from P-47D Maintenance Instruction)

Wartime, colour photo of P-47 D canopy.
(US National Archives)

Page 71 bottom: *Maj. John A. Carey, commander of 366th FG, 391st FS,. On D-Day+2, he landed on a partially completed airstrip on Normandy to pick up LT Calhoun who had crash-landed. Discarding his parachute, Carey sat in Calhoun's lap and flew them back to Thruxton. The unorthodox rescue earned Carey a dressing-down via telephone from Eisenhower — for risking his own aircraft — but it was clear that Ike admired Carey's daring act. He congratulated him on saving someone but said,* "Please don't do it again."
(US National Archives)

Canopy slid back. Armour plate is placed just behind the seat. The square hole was made in the museum.
(P. Wiśniewski)

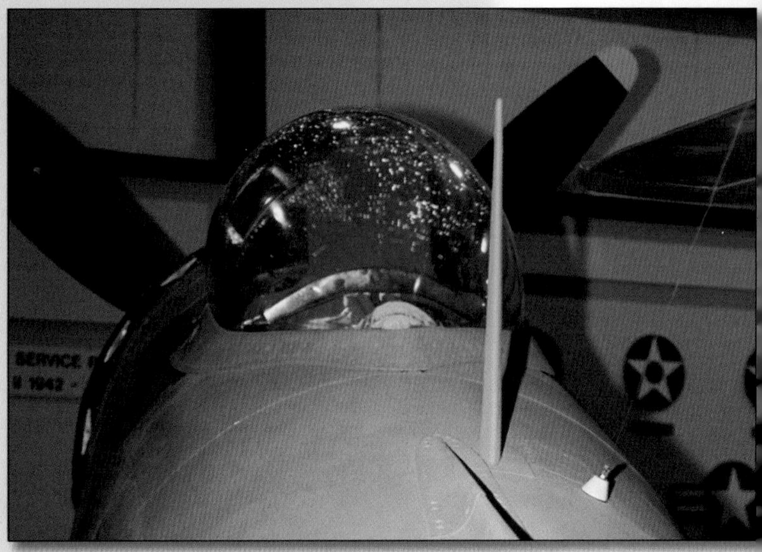

Canopy from the rear. The "bubble" shape is visible.
(P. Wiśniewski)

Two photos of the sliding bubble canopy, from the rear. Photos

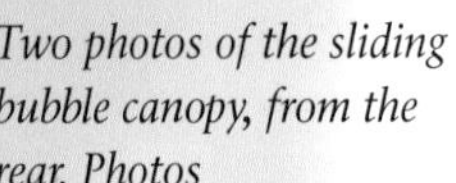

(P. Wiśniewski)
(J. Kightly)

Above: *The windscreen from the right. The front flat glass is bullet-proof to provide protection for the pilot.*
Below: *Canopy in open position from the left.*

(P. Wiśniewski)

COCKPIT

The instrument panel of the P-47D preserved in Brazil. (Guilherme Furtado Filho)

P-47D-28 instrument panel

1. Altimeter scale correction card
1. Propeller anti-icer control
2. Turbine overspeed warning light
3. Water pressure gauge line service
4. Altimeter
5. Turn indicator
6. Fuel level warning light
7. Airspeed indicator
8. Bank and turn indicator
9. Artificial horizon
10. Oil gauge line service
11. Suction gauge
12. Starter switch
13. Carburettor air temperature gauge
14. Master battery switch
15. Ignition switch
16. Turbo tachometer
17. Fuel quantity gauge
18. Hydraulic pressure gauge
19. Compass
20. Water pressure gauge
21. Rate of climb indicator
22. Manifold pressure gauge
23. Tachometer
24. Clock
25. Cylinder head temperature gauge
26. Fuel and oil pressure, oil temperature.

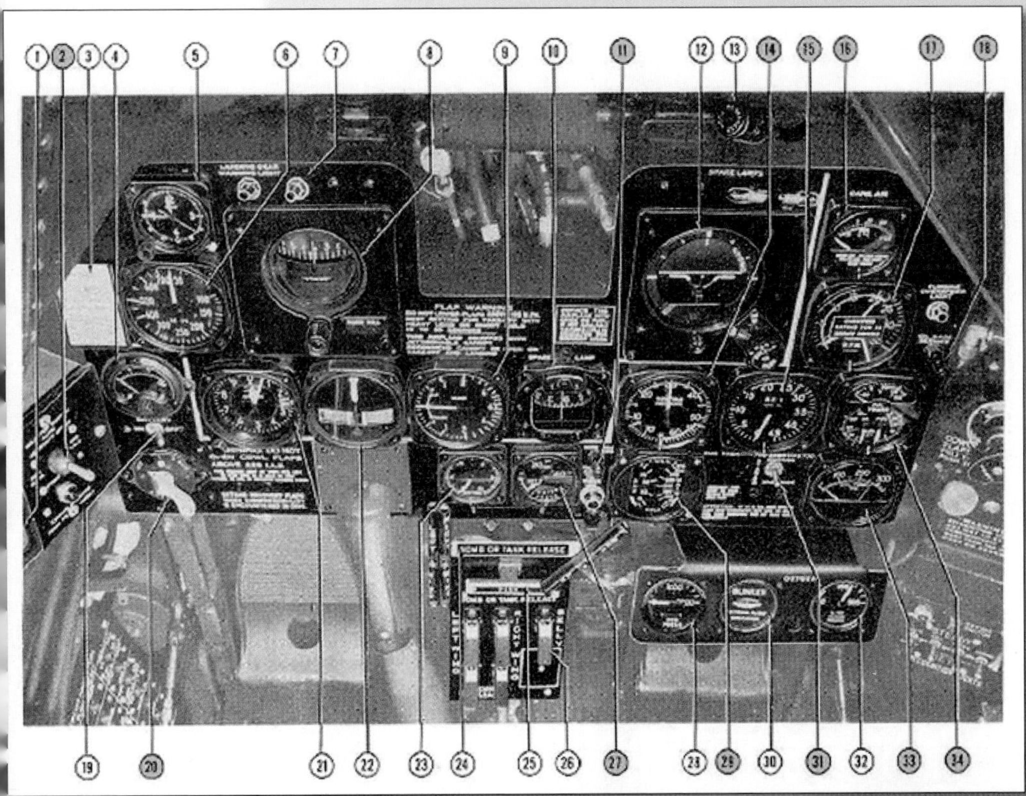

P-47D-30 instrument panel.
*1. Compressibility recovery flap switch
2. Propeller anti-icer control
3. Altimeeter scale correction card
4. Ammeter
5. Clock
6. Airspeed indicator
7. Landing gear warning light
8. Bank and turn indicator
9. Rate of climb indicator
10. Compass
11. Fuel pressure warning lamp
12. Artificial horizon
13. Defroster control
14. Manifold pressure gauge
15. Tachometer
16. Carburettor air temeperature gauge
17. Turbo tachometer
18. Hydraulic pressure gauge
19. Master battery switch
20. Ignition switch
21. Altimeter
22. Bank and turn indicator
23. Suction gauge
24. Bomb and tank release control
25. Parking brake control
26. Electric bomb and tank release selector panel
27. Water pressure gauge
28. Hydraulic pressure gauge
29. Fuel quantity gauge
30. Oxygen flow indicator
31. Starter switch
32. Oxygen cylinder pressure gauge
33. Cylinder head temperature gauge
34. Engine gauge unit.*

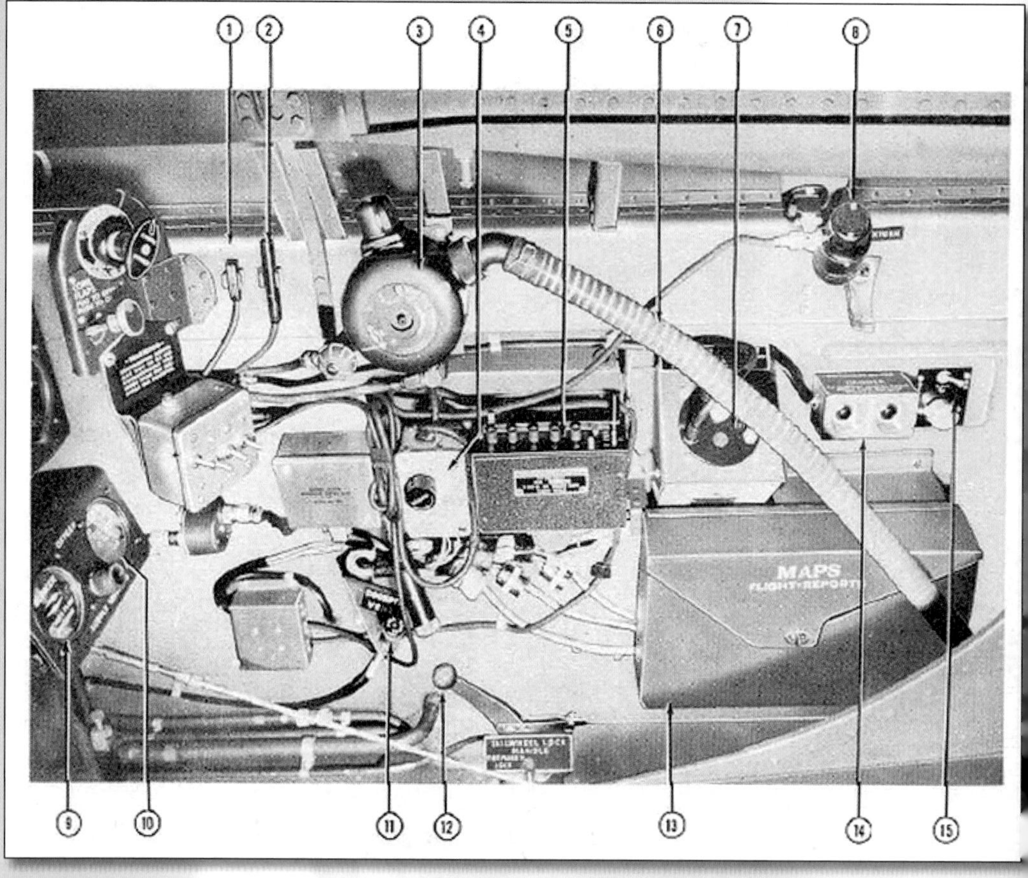

1. *Microphone connector plug*
2. *Headphone connector plug*
3. *Oxygen regulator*
4. *Radio receiver volume control*
5. *Control box assembly*
6. *Oxygen feeder hose*
7. *Beam receiver*
8. *Cockpit light*
9. *Oxygen flow indicator*
10. *Oxygen pressure gauge*
11. *Cockpit vent control*
12. *Tail wheel lock*
13. *(MAP) case*
14. *Secret radio detonator*
15. *Secret radio switch*

Above: *Starboard side of the P-47D cockpit. Photo from the Pilot's Manual.*
Below: *Photo of preserved P-47D.*

(P. Wiśniewski)

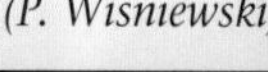

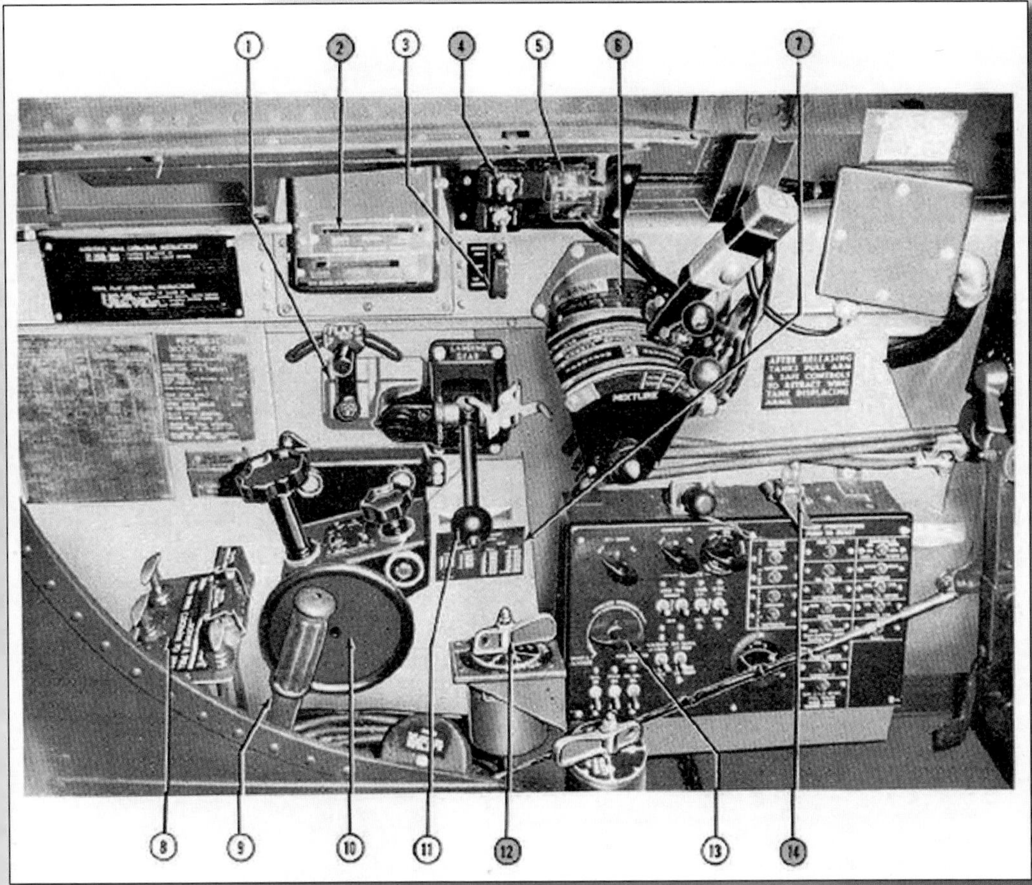

Portside of the P-47D cockpit. Photo from the Pilot's Manual.

1. Wing flap control handle
2. Intercooler and oilcooler shutter indicator
3. Gun safety switch
4. Intercooler and oilcooler shutter switches
5. Canopy switch
6. Engine control quadrant
7. Three point fuel correction chart
8. External tank and bomb release
9. Hydraulic hand pump
10. Trim tab control unit.
11. Landing gear control
12. Main fuel selector valve
13. Fuel booster pump rheostat
14. Landing gear warning switch

Figure 6—Engine Control Quadrant

1. Water Injection Switch
2. Throttle Lever
3. Push-to-talk Button
4. Supercharger Control
5. Propeller Control
6. Mixture Control
7. Take-Off Stop

P-47D engine instruments.

1. Tachometer

2. Manifold pressure gauge

4. Carburettor air temp. gauge.

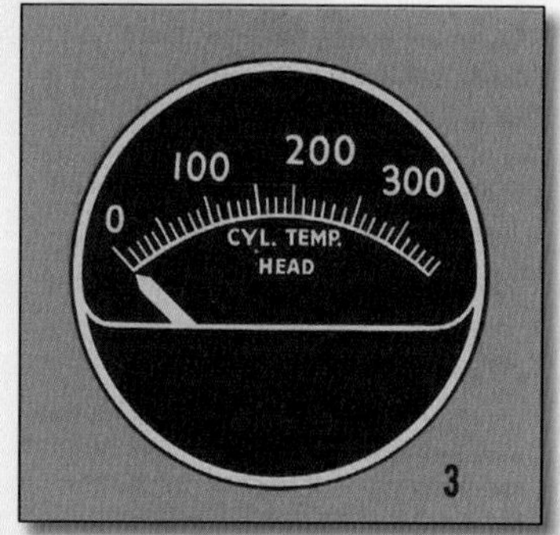

3. Cylinder head temp. gauge

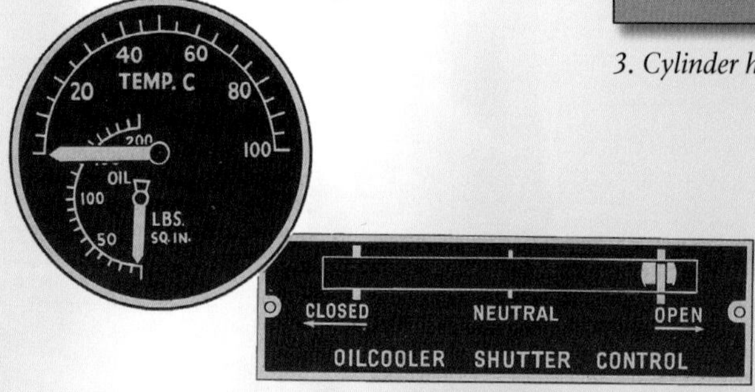

5. Oil pressure indicator
6. Oil temp. indicator.

All drawings from the Pilot's Manual

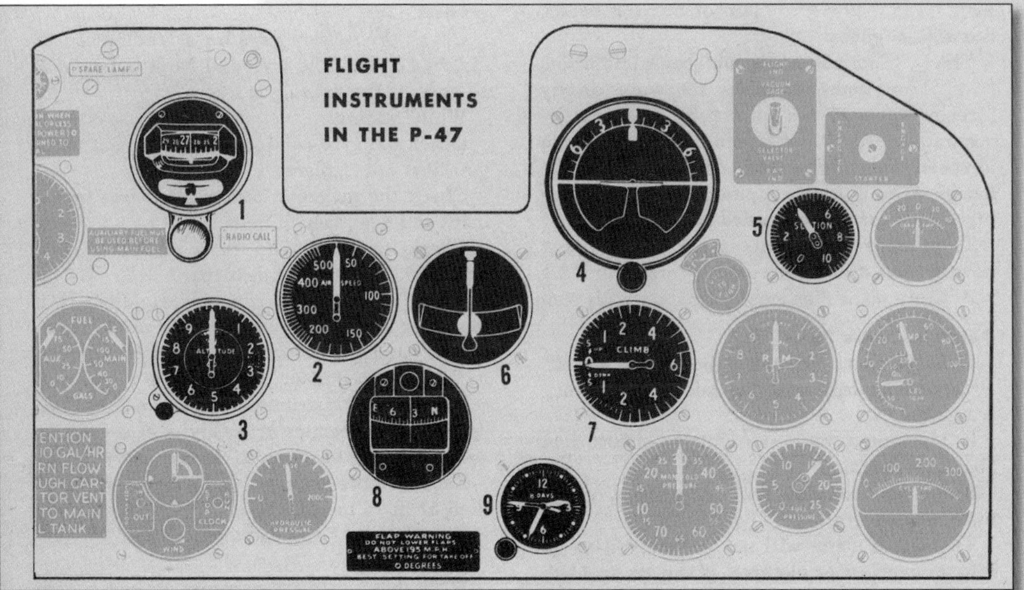

Above: *P-47D-25 flight instruments. (Drawing from the Pilot's Manual)*
Below: *Instrument panel of preserved P-47D in Brazil. Note different location of some instruments.*
(Guilherme Furtado Filho)

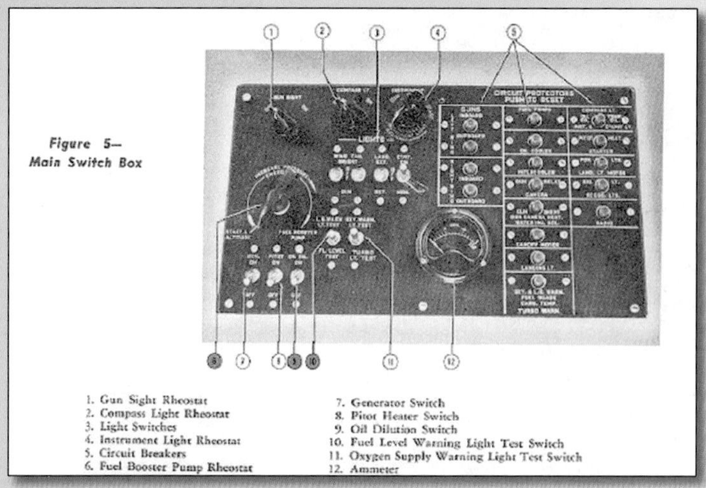

Above: P-47D Main switch box located at the portside cockpit wall.

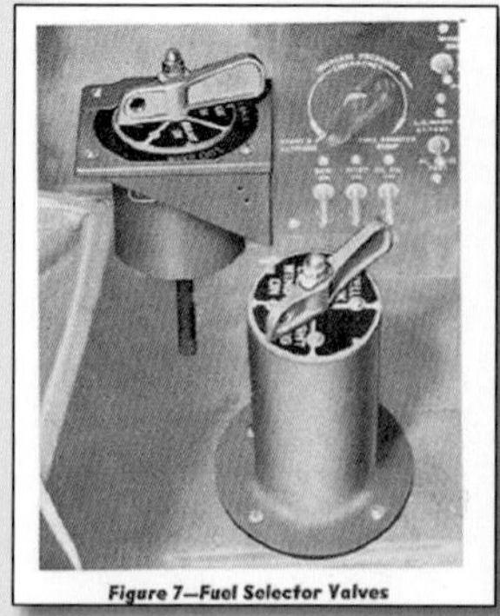
Figure 7—Fuel Selector Valves

P-47D Fuel selector valves located on the portside cockpit wall.

Below: N-3B gunsight assembly, used on P-47D-25. Drawing from P-47D Maintenence instructions.

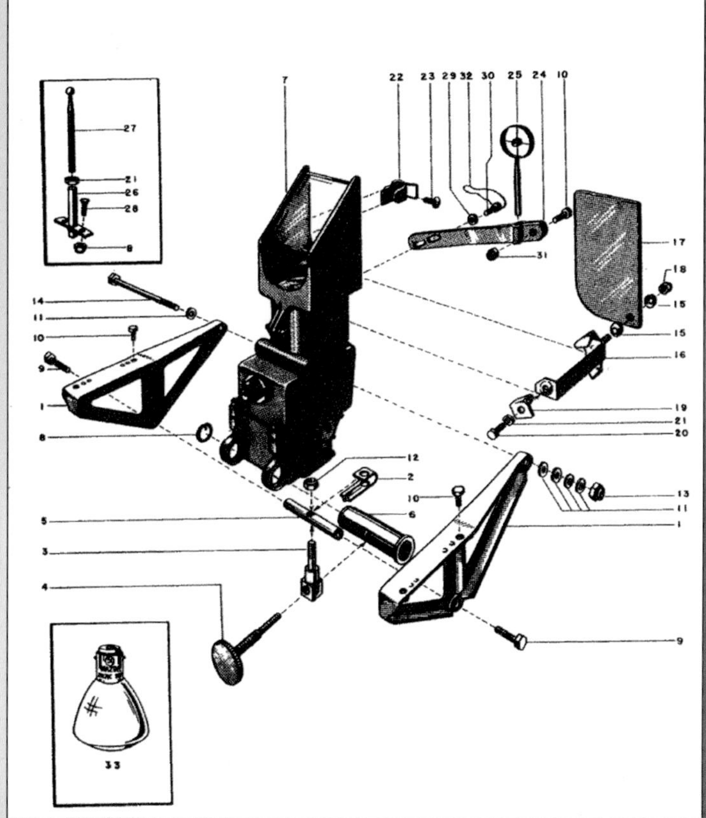

Below: Contactor clock.

Below: Electric propeller switches located on the portside wall.

Figure 4—Electric Propeller Switches

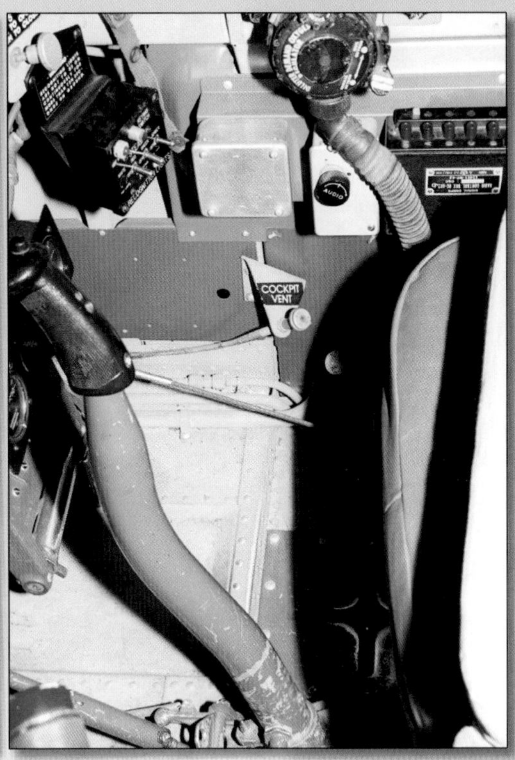

Left photos: *Details of Mark VIII gunsight.*
Above: *Control column as used in all P-47Ds.*
Below: *The top of the pilot's armour is visible. Note that the pilot's headrest is removed.*
(All photos P. Wiśniewski)

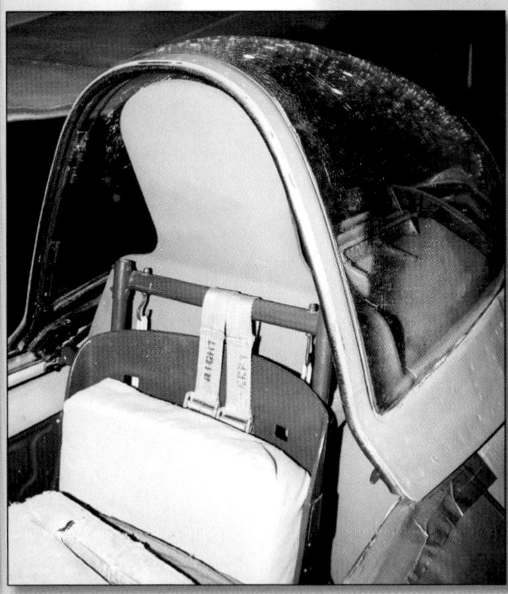

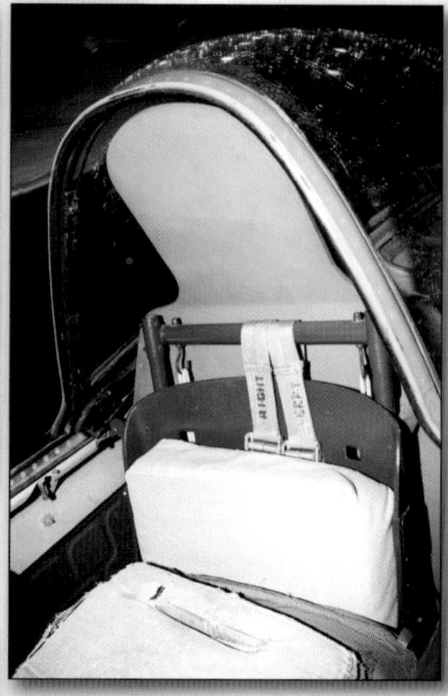

Above: Pilot's armoured headrest.

Above: left: Instrument panel from the left.

Left: Mark VIII gunsight mount.

Below: K-14 gyro gunsight, from the left. This gunsight was introduced on the D-40 variant.

(All photos P. Wiśniewski)

From the top:
The floor of early P-47D, with corrugations.
(R. Pęczkowski)

The floor of P-47D-40 without corrugations, also used in P-47M.
(P. Przymusiała)

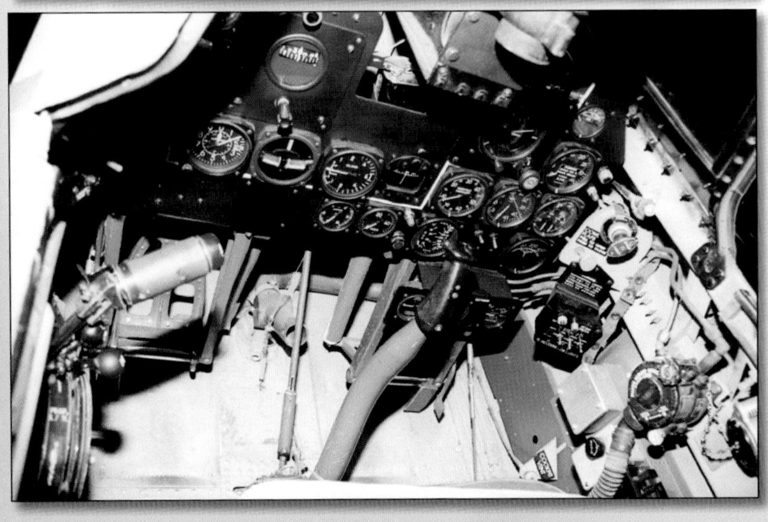

Lower part of the instrument panel. Also rudder pedals are visible.
(P. Wiśniewski)

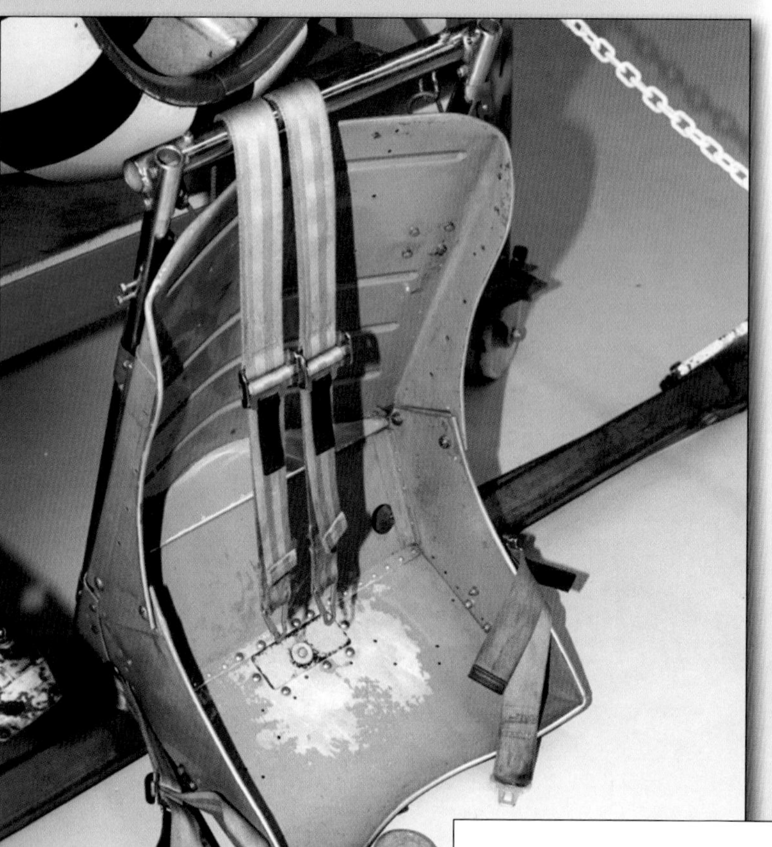

Pilot's seat.
(P. Wiśniewski)

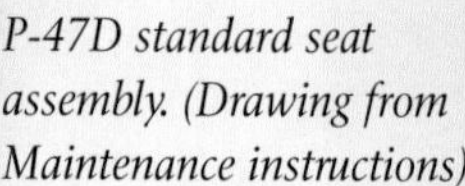

P-47D standard seat assembly. (Drawing from Maintenance instructions)

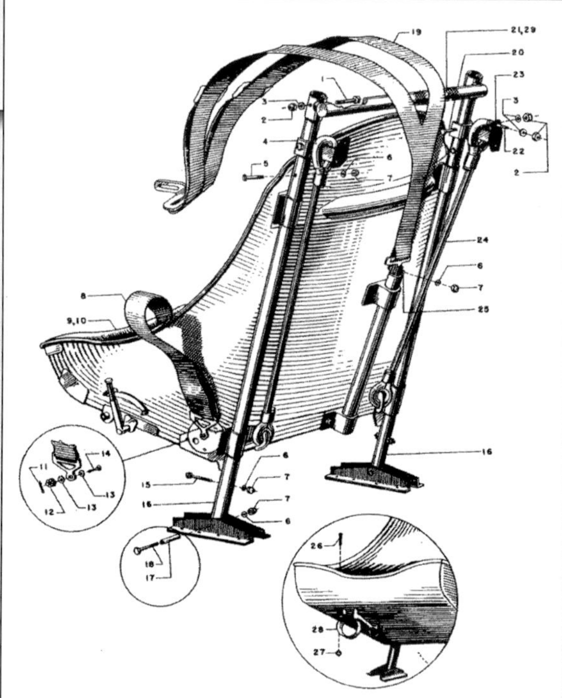

INSTRUMENT PANEL

P-47N instrument panel.

1. Ammeter
2. Airspeed Indicator
3. Clock
4.Altimeter
5. Landing Gear Warning Light
6 Tail warning light
7. Bank and turn idicator
8. Directional Gyro Indicator
9. (Deleted)
10. K-14B Gunsight
11. Compass
12. Artificial Horizon Indicator
13. Manifold Pressure Gauge
14. Tachometer
15. Carburetor Air Temperature Gauge
16.Fuel and oil pressure and oil temp. gauge
17. Defroster control
18. Internal wing fuel and oil quantity gages.
19. Battery switch
20. Ignition Switch
21. Armament Selector Panel
22. Accelerometer
23. Manual bomb releases
24. Suction gauge
25. Parking brake
26. Rocket Selector Panel
27. Water pressure gauge
28. Main tank fuel level warning light
29. Cylinder Head Temperature Gauge
30. Hydraulic Pressure Gauge
31. Engine Primer Switch
32. Starter Switch
33. Main and auxilliary tank fuel gages.
34. Oxygen Pressure Gauge (Earlier versions contain a turbo tachometer and warning light.

Below: *Ammeter.*

Top, left: *Autopilot control & Tachometer.*

Top, right: *Carburetor Air Temperature Gauge*

Second row: *Directional Gyro Indicator & Artificial Horizon Indicator*

Third row: *Accelerometer & Rocket Selector Panel*

Bottom: *Oxygen Pressure Gauges*

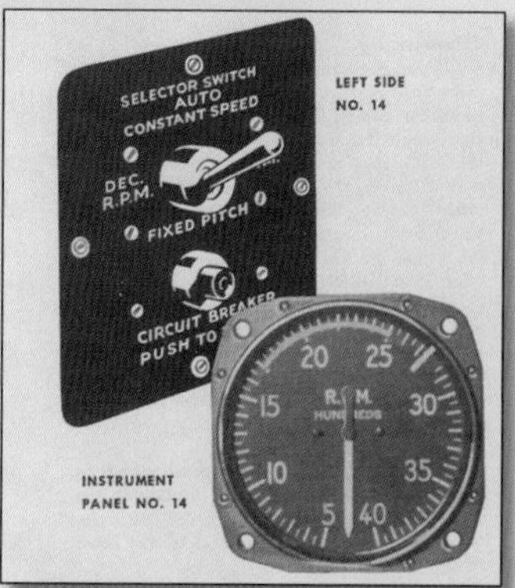

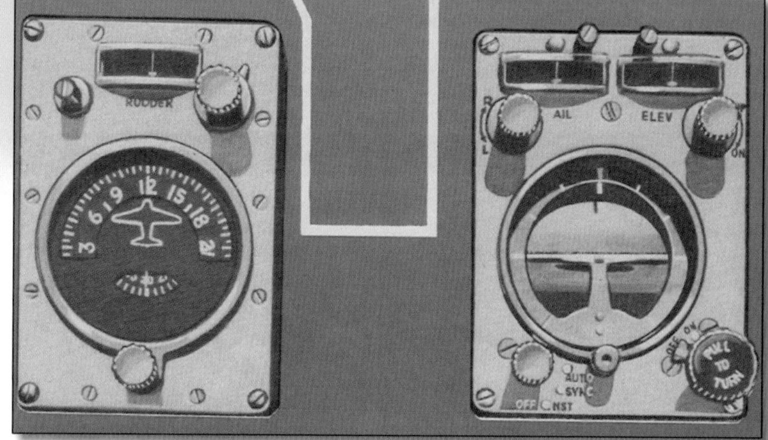

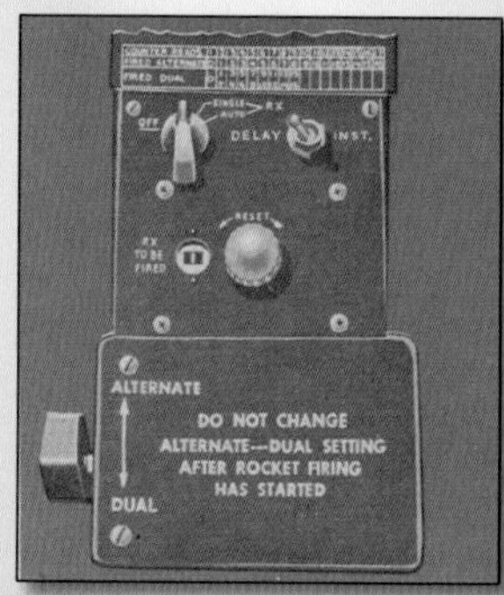

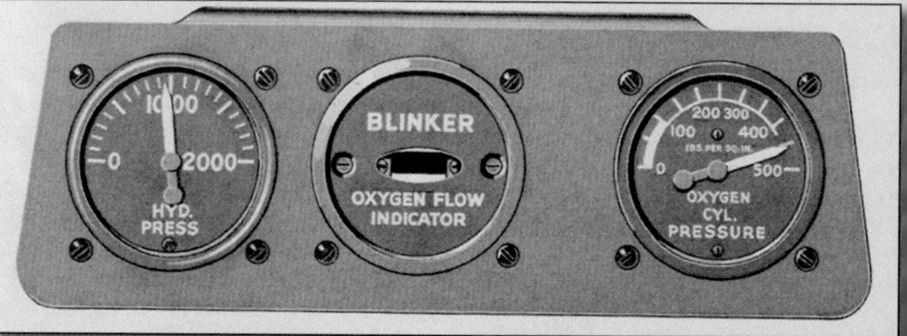

Top, left: *Fuel and oil pressure and oil temp. gauge.*

Top, right: *Internal wing fuel and oil quantity gauges.*

Middle, left: *Main and auxiliary tank fuel gauges.*

Middle, right: *Water pressure gauge.*

Tail warning radar.

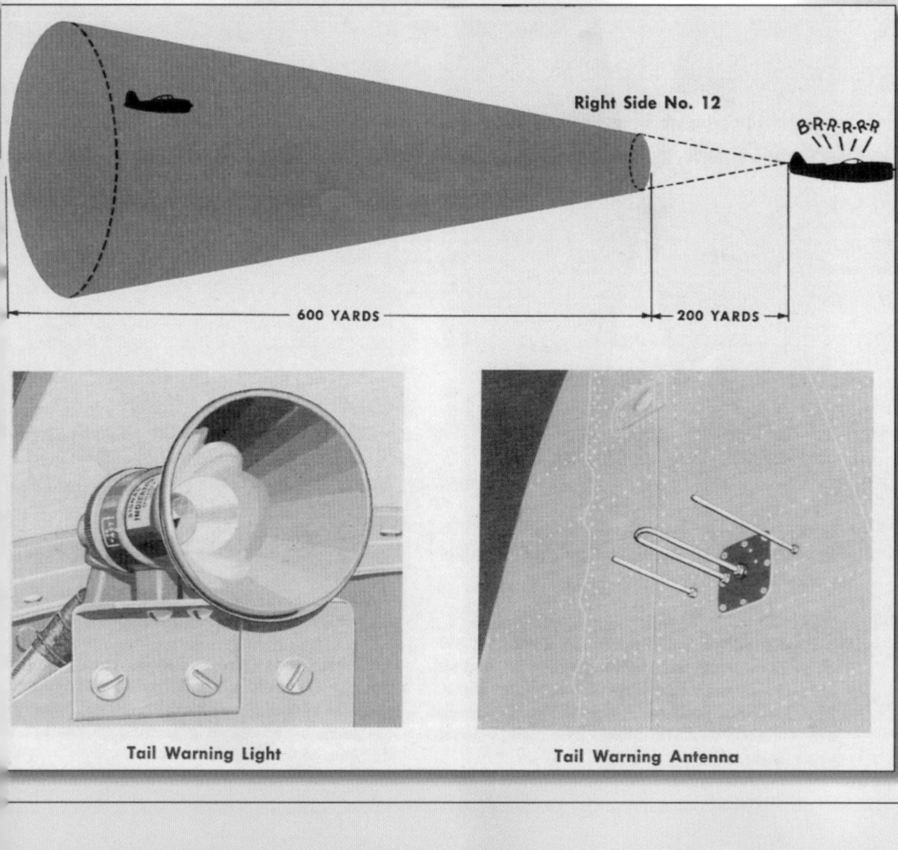

Right Side No. 12

B-R-R-R-R-R

600 YARDS

200 YARDS

Tail Warning Light

Tail Warning Antenna

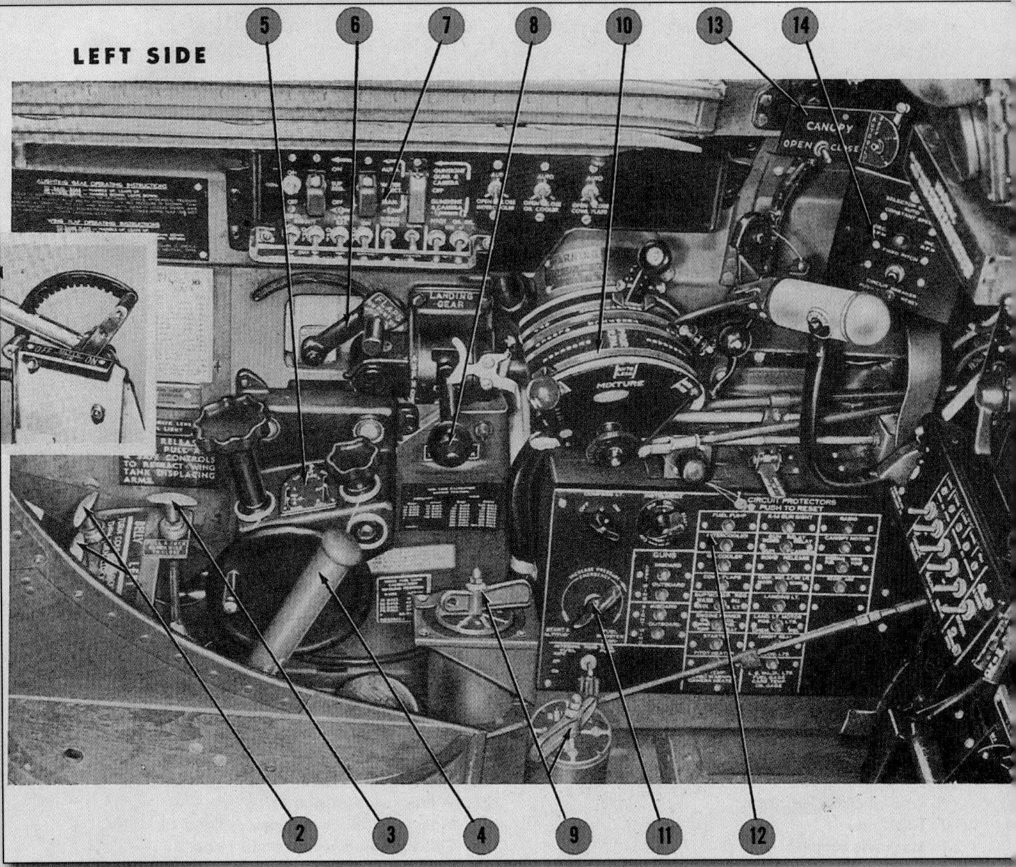

LEFT SIDE

P-47N portside cockpit wall. Photo from the Pilot's Manual.

1. Air filter control
2. Bomb arming handles
3. Gunbay heat control
4. Manual hydraulic pump
5. Trim Tab Control Unit
6. Flap control
7. Main Switch Panel
8. Landing Gear Control
9. Fuel Selector Valves
10. Throttle quadrant
11. Fuel booster pump rheostat
12. Circuit Protector Panel
13. Propeller Switch Box
14. Autopilot ON-OFF control

Below: *Throttle quadran. 1. Boost control; 2. Throttle, the twist grip is used for ranging K-14 gunsight, button turns on the microphone; 3. Propeller control; 4. Mixture control; 5. Tension knob.*

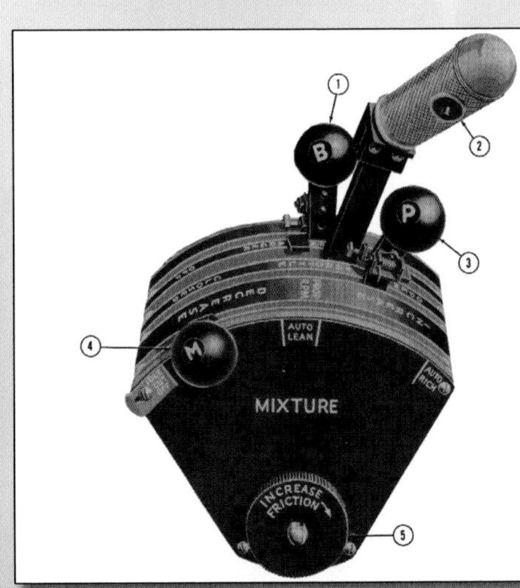

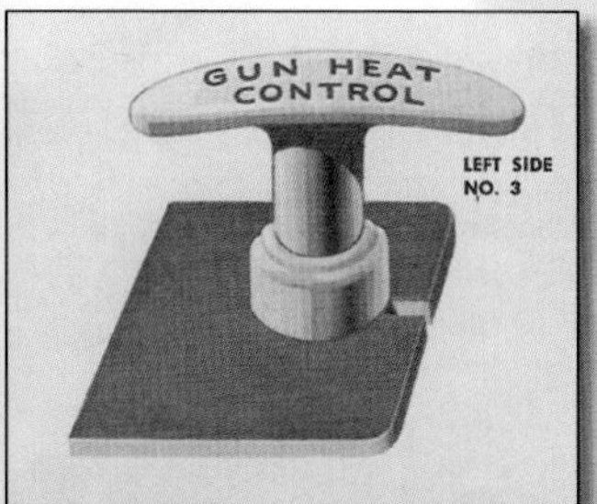

Top, left: Gunbay heat control.

Top, right: Bomb arming handles.

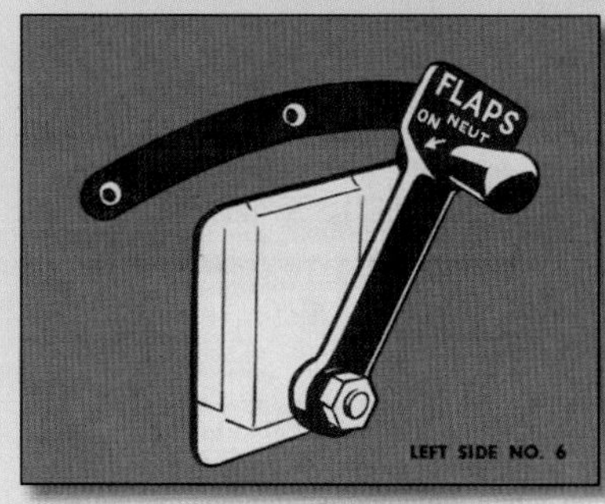

Middle, left: Landing Gear Control.

Middle, right: Flap control.

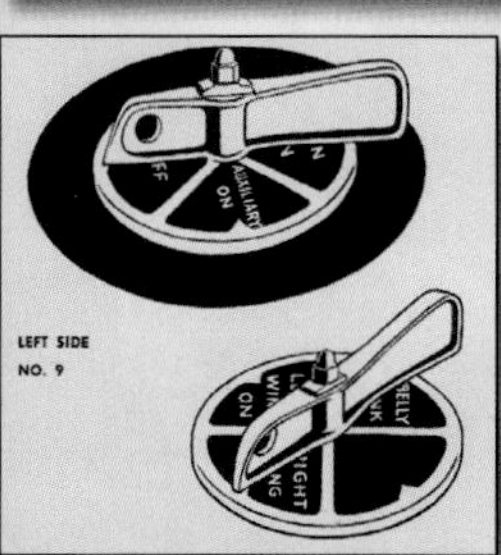

Left: Fuel Selector Valves.

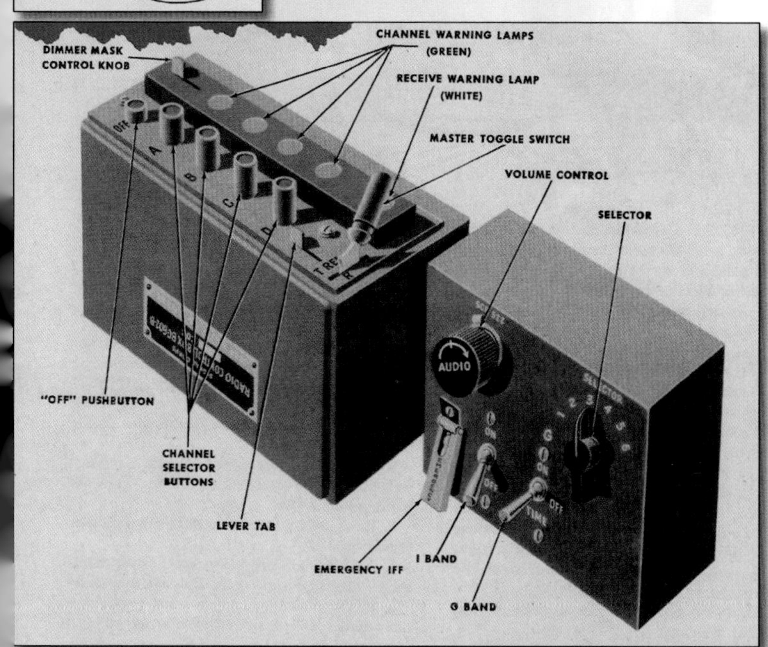

Left: Radio equipment.

Above: *P-47N starboard wall. Photo from Pilot's Manual.*
Below, left: *SCR-695A Radio Controls.*
Below, right: *AN/ARC-3 (IFF) controls.*

1.Recognition Lights Switch Box
2. VHF radio
3. Oxygen regulator
4. Cockpit ventilator control
5. Flare gun adapter
6. Tailwheel lock
7. AN/ARC-3 (IFF) controls
8. SCR-695A Radio Controls
9. Secret Radio Detonator
10. Cockpit Swivel Ligh
11. BC-453B or E Radio Control
12. Tail warning switch box
13. Manual canopy handle.

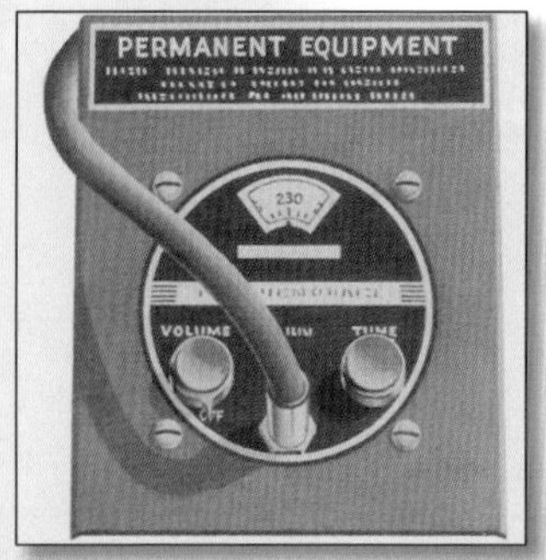

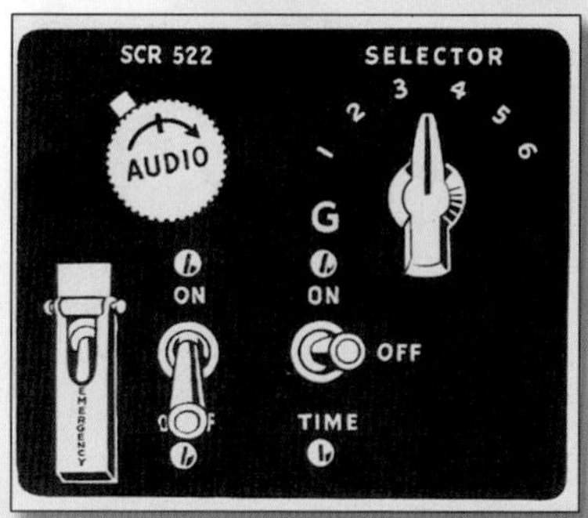

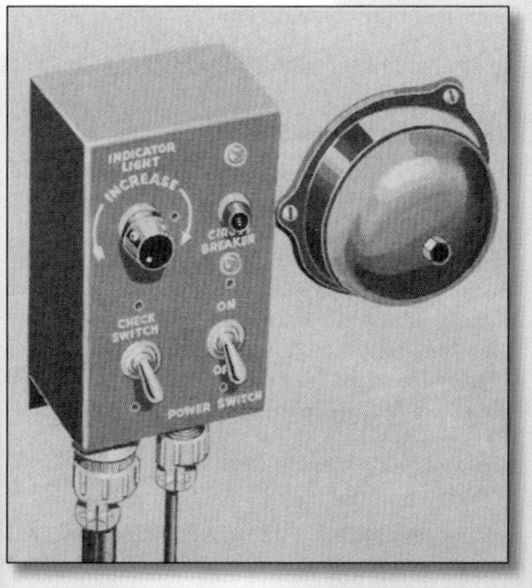

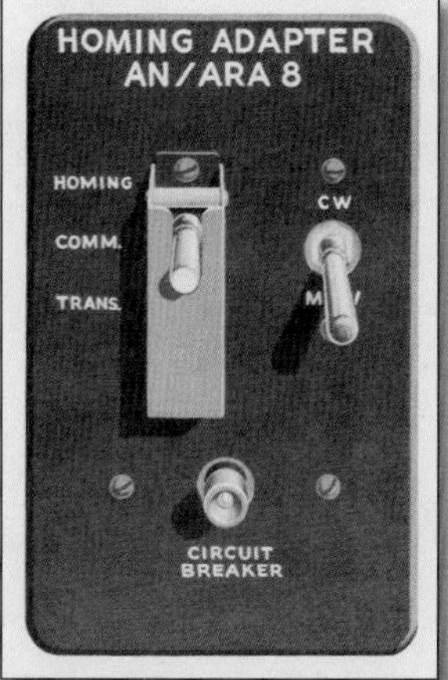

Top, left: *Tail warning switch box.*

Top, right: *BC-453B or E Radio Control*

Bottom: *K-14 Gunsight.*

1. Reflector plate
2. Span dial
3. Range dial
4. Lamp cover
5. Light rheostat
6. Selector switch.

K-14 Gunsight

INSTRUMENT PANEL NO. 10

1
2
3
4
5
6

P-47N--15 changes. Microphone button was moved to the end of the throttle control. Electrical bomb arming. Light rheostat and sight selector of the gunsight were moved to the left side of the cockpit.

(Photos from P-47N Pilot's Manual)

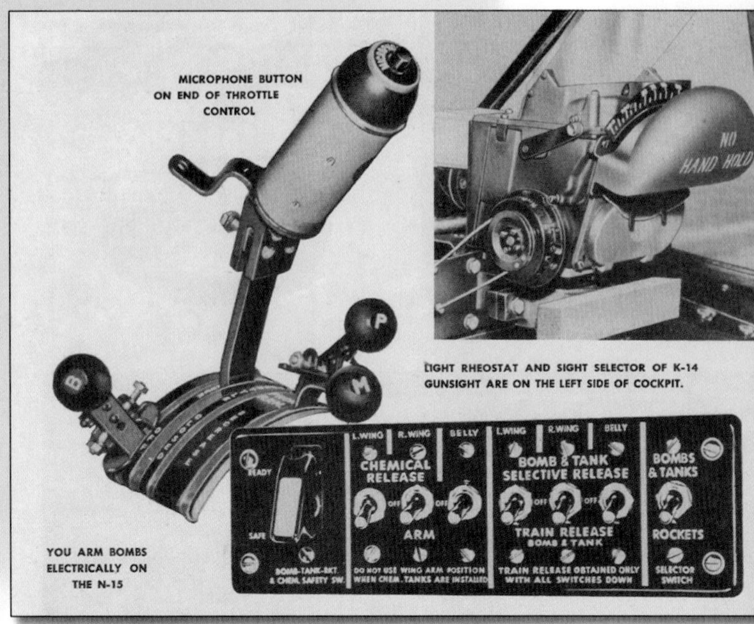

AUTOMATIC ENGINE CONTROL

ALTERNATE FEED

STREAMLINED RIGHT SIDE OF COCKPIT

***Right**: P-47N-25 changes. N-25 is equipped with Automatic Engine Control, which automatically maintains a correct boost and throttle relationship. The starboard side of the cockpit has been streamlined by rearrangement of the radio equipment. VHF radio is equipped with 8 channels. Also N-25 has an alternate feed to get petrol from the internal wing tanks.*

(P-47N Pilot's Manual)

Above: Col. F. Gabreski is wearing standard helmet, gloves and oxygen mask.

(US National Archives)

Below: Lt Irving Ostuw of 368th FG, 396th FS in Germany 1945.

(Kenneth Kik)

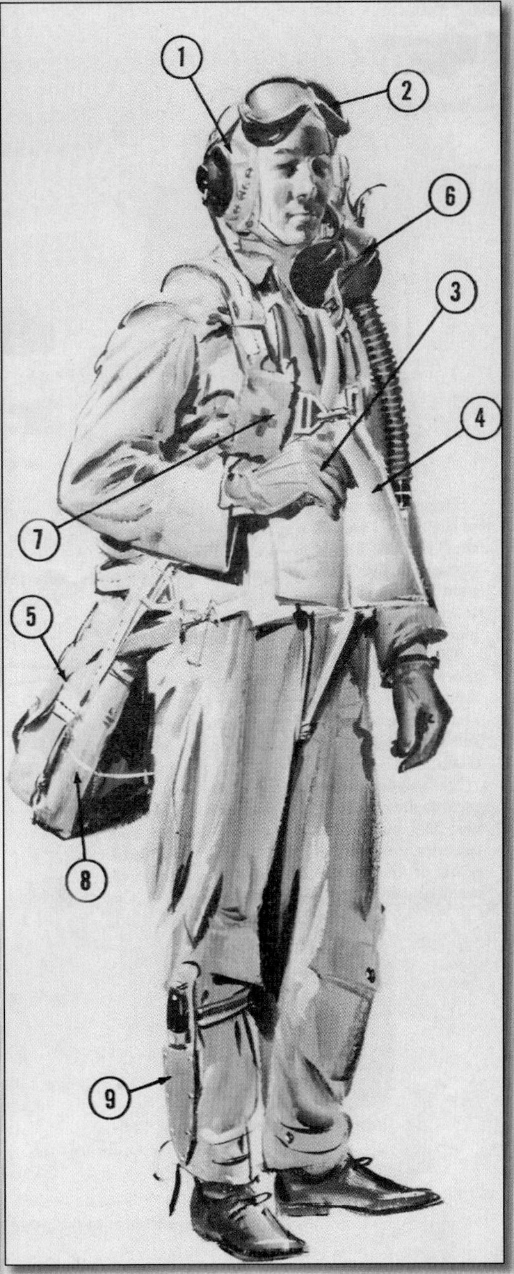

Personal equipment.

(Drawing from the P-47N Pilot's Manual)

1. Helmet; 2. Goggles; 3. Gloves; 4. Life vest; 5. Parachute; 6. Oxygen mask; 7. First aid emergency kit; 8. One-man life raft (when flying over water); 9. Knife.

TAIL

Above and right: Tail of P-47D-40-RA.

Right: Tail of the P-47N.

(All photos P. Wiśniewski)

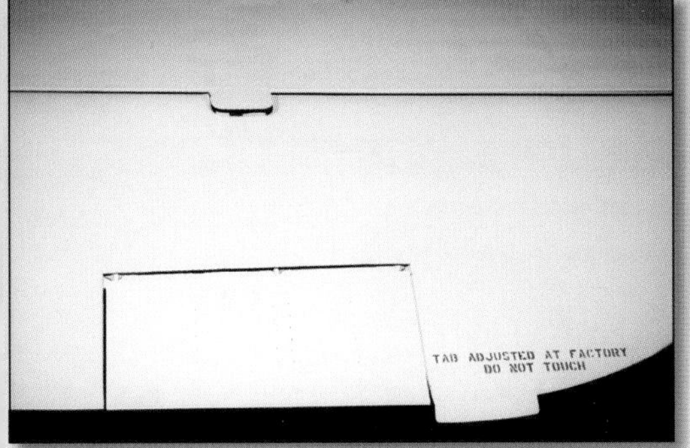

Photos of the rudder and elevator of P-47D.
(P. Wiśniewski, R. Pęczkowski)

More tail photos.
(Guilherme Furtado Filho),
(R. Pęczkowski),
(P. Przymusiała),
(via P. Skulski)

Left:
P-47D port elevator in up position.
(P. Skulski)

Left: *P-47D rudder from the left.*

Below:
The trim tab of the port elevator. Note that there are two trim tabs. One is movable in flight and the second one is fixed.
(G. Papadimitriou via P. Skulski)

Photos of the P-47N tail. P-47N-25-RE, serial 44-89348 displayed as HV-A at Lackland Air Force Base, Texas. (All photos P. Wiśniewski)

ENGINE

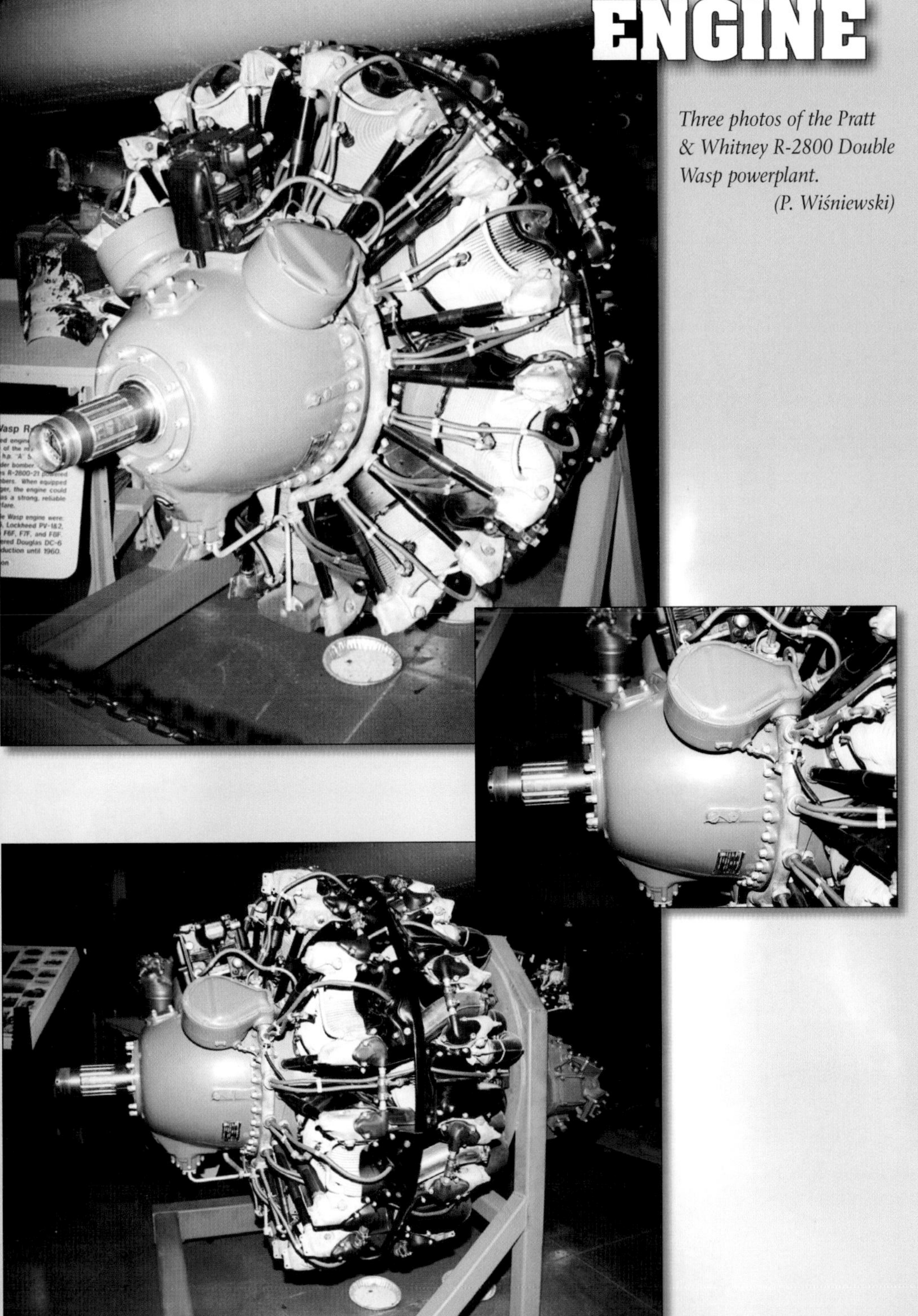

Three photos of the Pratt & Whitney R-2800 Double Wasp powerplant.
(P. Wiśniewski)

***Above**: P-47D with all engine panels removed.*

(US National Archives)

***Below**: Engine mount frame and electrical installation.*

(Drawing from Maintenance Instructions)

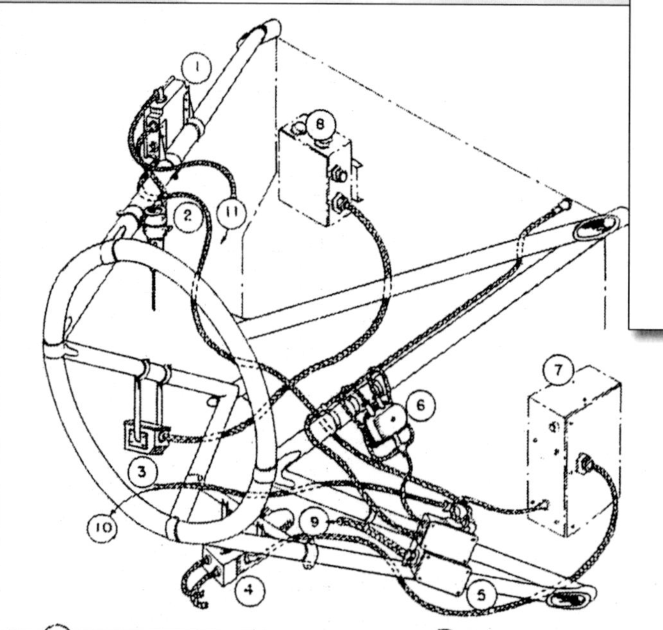

***Above:** Engine cylinder.*
(Drawing from Maintenance Instructions)

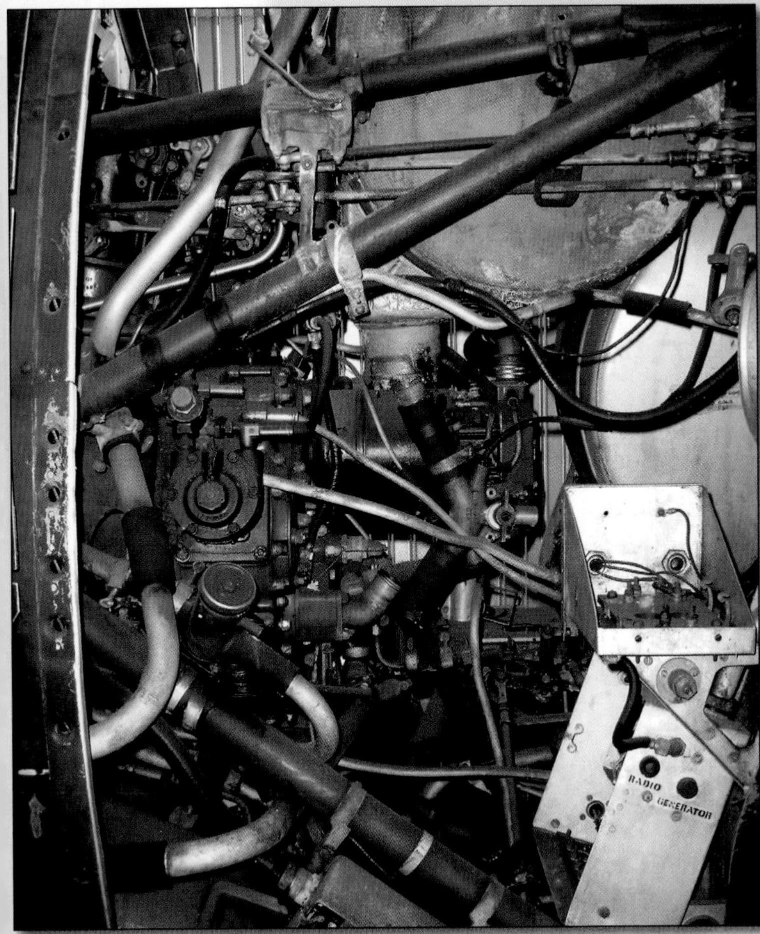

Above:
R-2800 engine from the rear.
(Guilherme Furtado Filho)

Left:
Two photos of the R-2800 engine details. The oil tank is clearly visible in the lower photo.
(G. Nowakowski via P. Skulski)

R-2800 engine assembly. (Drawing from Maintenance Instructions)

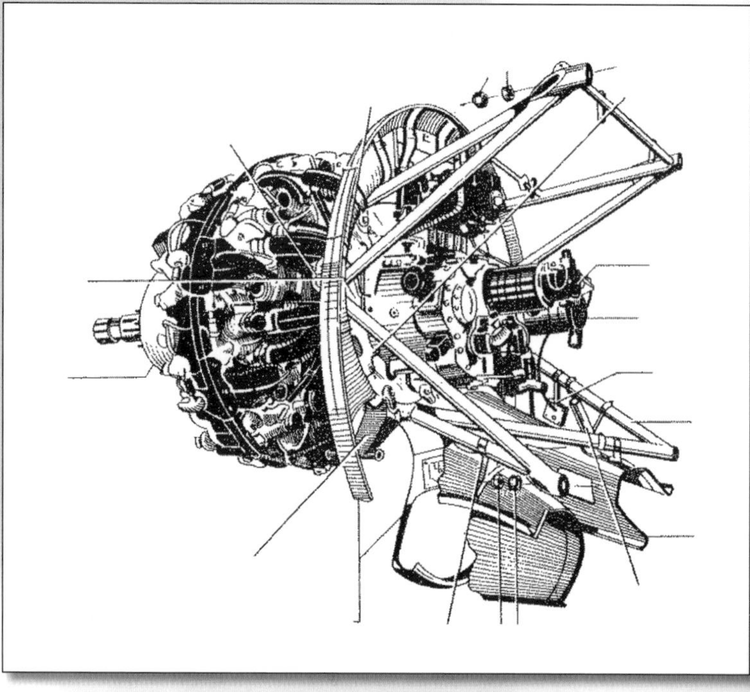

R-2800 powerplant cylinders.

(G. Nowakowski via P. Skulski)

Front view of P-47D during engine overhaul.
(Chris Barnes)

P-47D engine exhaust system.
(Drawing from Maintenance Instructions)

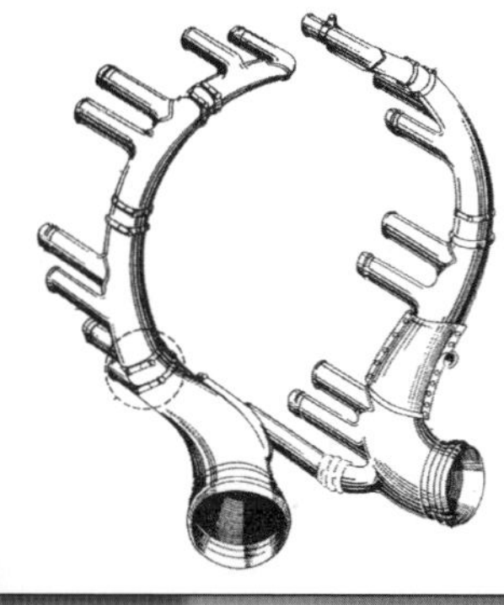

Oil cooler details.
(P. Wiśniewski)

P-47D, "The Wolf" s/n unknown of 368th FG, 395th FS. (Kenneth Kik)

Two photos of P-47D engine cowling.
(R. Peczkowski & G. Papadimitriou)

Engine cowling of P-47D (s/n unknown), "Section 8" from 358th FG, 397th FS.
(Kenneth Kik)

Three photos showing the oil cooler door and the exhaust waste gate. The exhaust gate is located aft of the oil cooler door and between the door and the exhaust is a fixed deflector.

(G. Papadimitriou via P. Skulski)

Front view of the engine with all panels removed. Note that port oil cooler is removed also.
(R. Pęczkowski)

***Left:** Front view of the engine cowling.*

***Below, left:** The rear of the engine cowling*
(R. Pęczkowski)

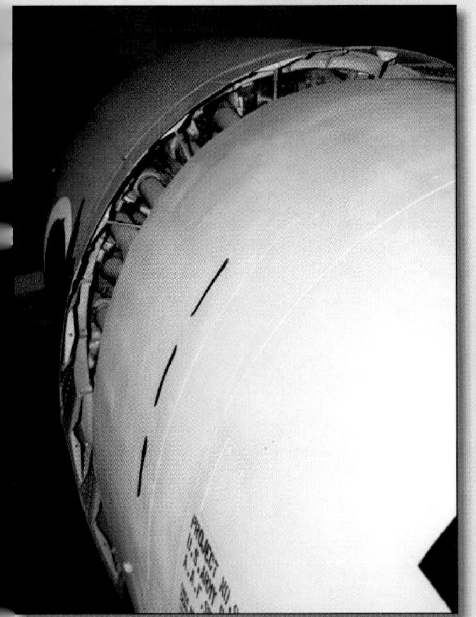

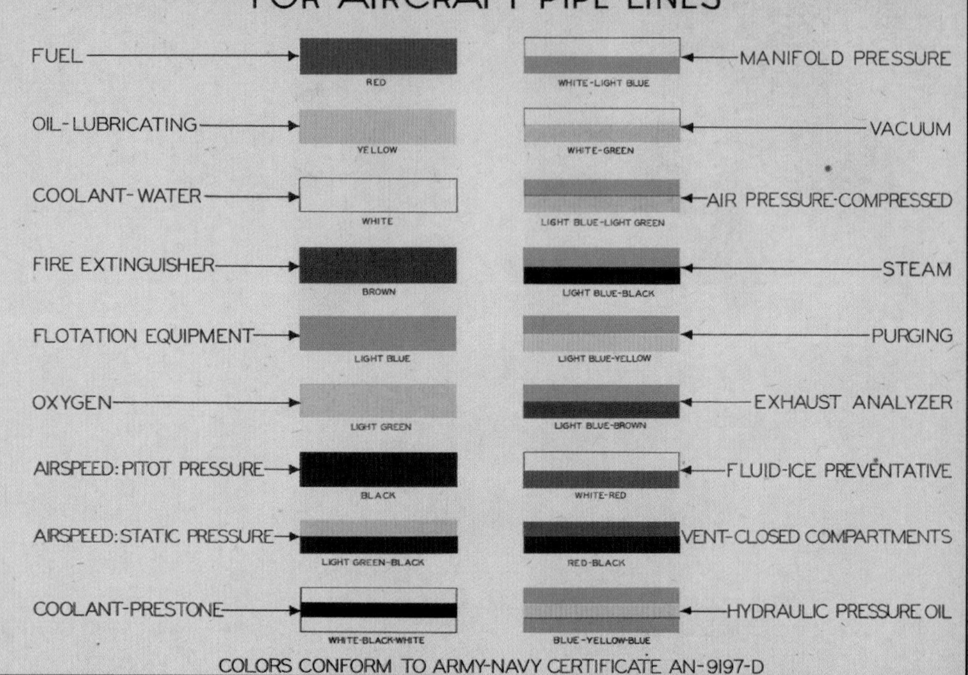

Above: Colour coding for aircraft pipe lines. Offical USAAF chart.
(Drawing from Engine Manual)

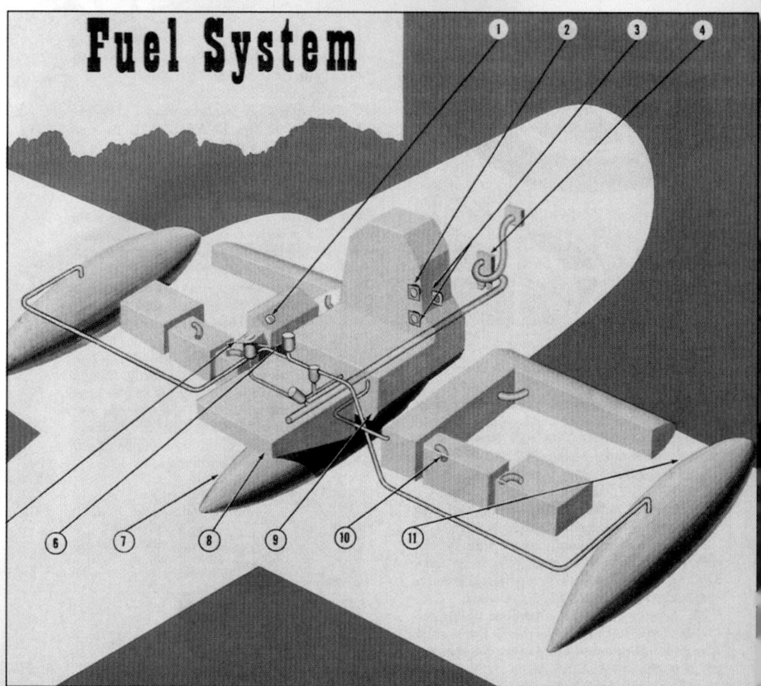

Right: P-47D fuel system.
(Darwing from Pilot's Manual)

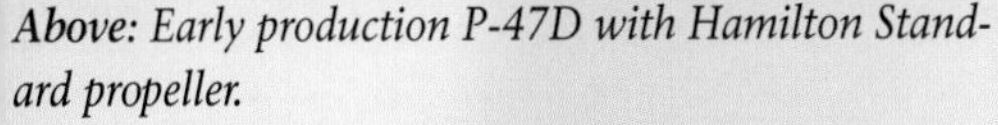

Above: *Early production P-47D with Hamilton Standard propeller.*

(US National Archives)

Above: *Working on P-47D, "Burning Desire" of 86th FBG, 525th FS in Corsica, 1944. Personal aircraft of Ken Barnes. Aircraft is equipped with symetrical blades Curstiss Electric propeller.*
This plane took part in Operation Dragoon, the invasion of the South of France. "Burning Desire" got hit in the wing, cracked up upon an emergency landing and burned, in November, 1944.

(Chris Barnes)

Colour wartime photo of Brasilian P-47D. Aircraft with Hamilton Standard propeller.

(US National Archives)

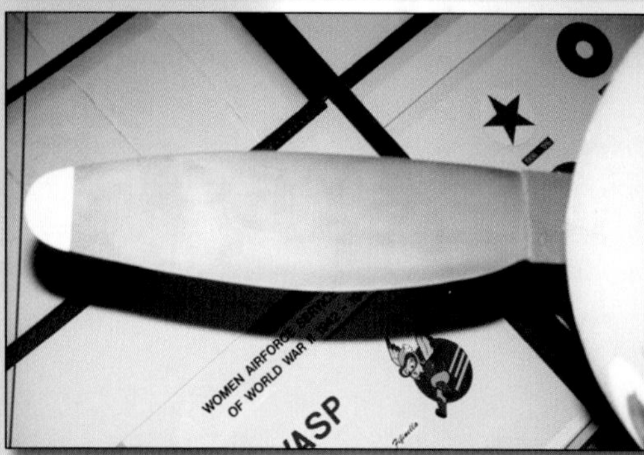

Above left: *Blade of Hamilton-Standard Hydromatic propeller.*
Above: *The hub of Hamilton-Standard propeller.*
Left: *Asymmetrical Curtiss Electric paddle-blade propeller, from the rear.*
Below left: *Symmetrical Curtiss Electric paddle-blade propeller, from the rear.*
Below: *The hub of Curtiss Electric propeller.*
Photos (P. Wiśniewski, R. Pęczkowski)

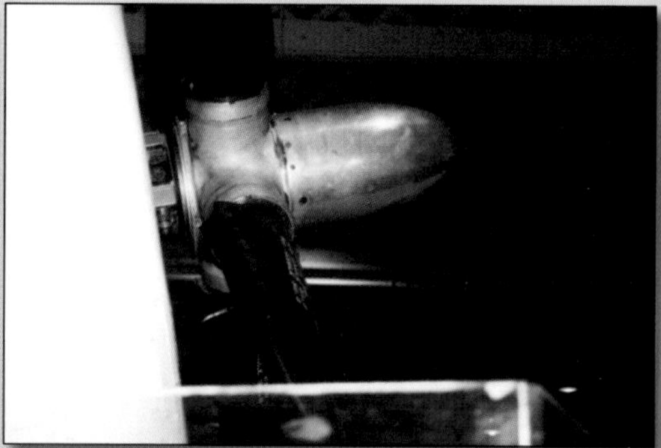

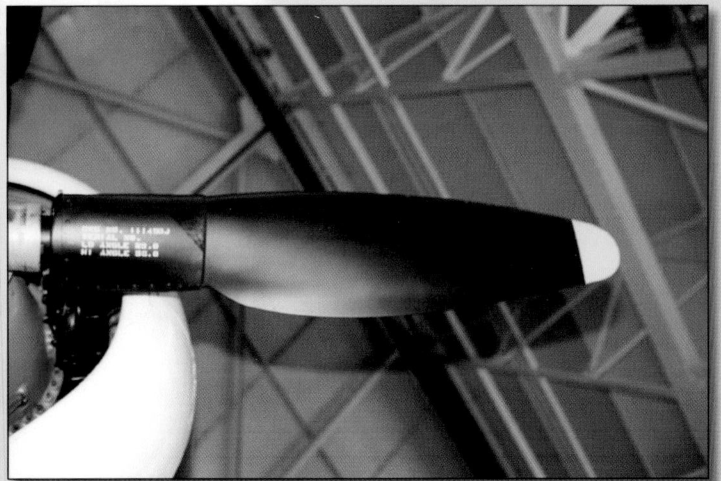

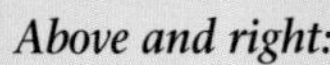

Above and right:
Three photos showing the details of the asymmetrical Curtiss Electric paddle-blade

Left and below:
Two photos of the Curtiss Electric hub.

Photos: (P. Wiśniewski), (R. Pęczkowski), (via S. Skulski)

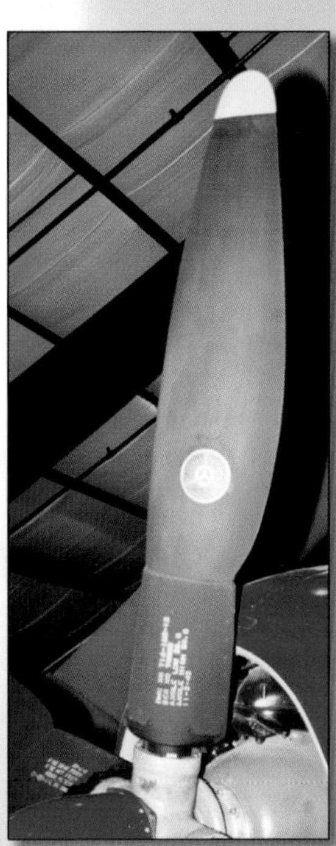

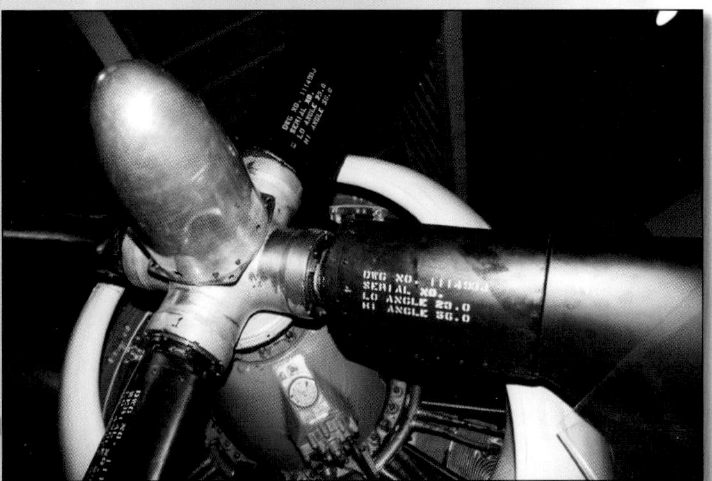

UNDERCARRIAGE

Above:
Front views of the port and starboard main undercarriage.
(P. Wiśniewski)

Right:
Main undercarriage arrangement. The asymmetrical Curtiss Electric paddle-blade propeller is also visible.
(M. Orlog)

RIB STATIONS
DOOR CYLINDER "J"
DOWNLOCK (B)
26
40
52
64
74
86
104
VALVE PUSH ROD "G"
PIVOT POINT
SHRINKAGE STRUT
"E" RETRACTING CYLINDER
"K" WHEEL DOOR
"F" SHOCK STRUT
EXTENDED VIEW
UP LOCK "H"
26
40
52
64
74
86
104
DOOR LOCK "L"
PIVOT POINT
"J" DOOR RETRACTING CYLINDER
RETRACTED VIEW

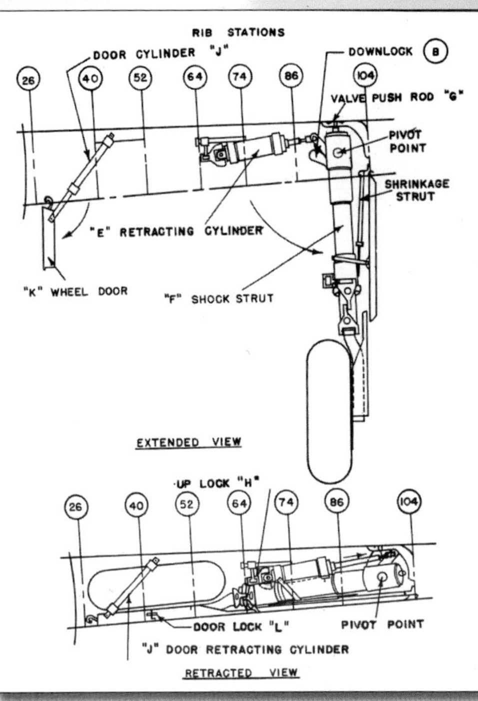

Drawings of the P-47D undercarriage from Maintenance Instructions.

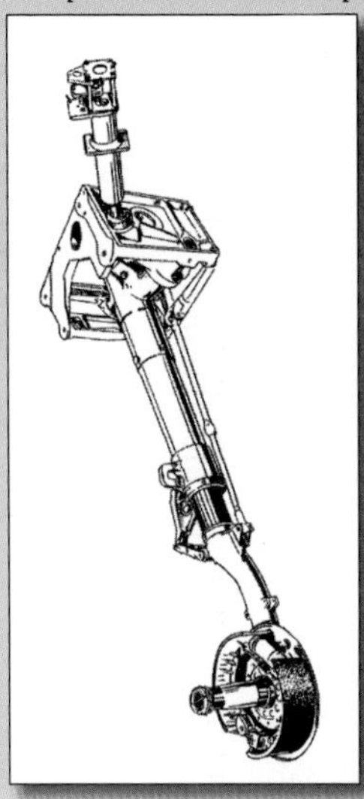

P-47D-25 Hydraulic System.
(Drawing from the Pilot's Manual)

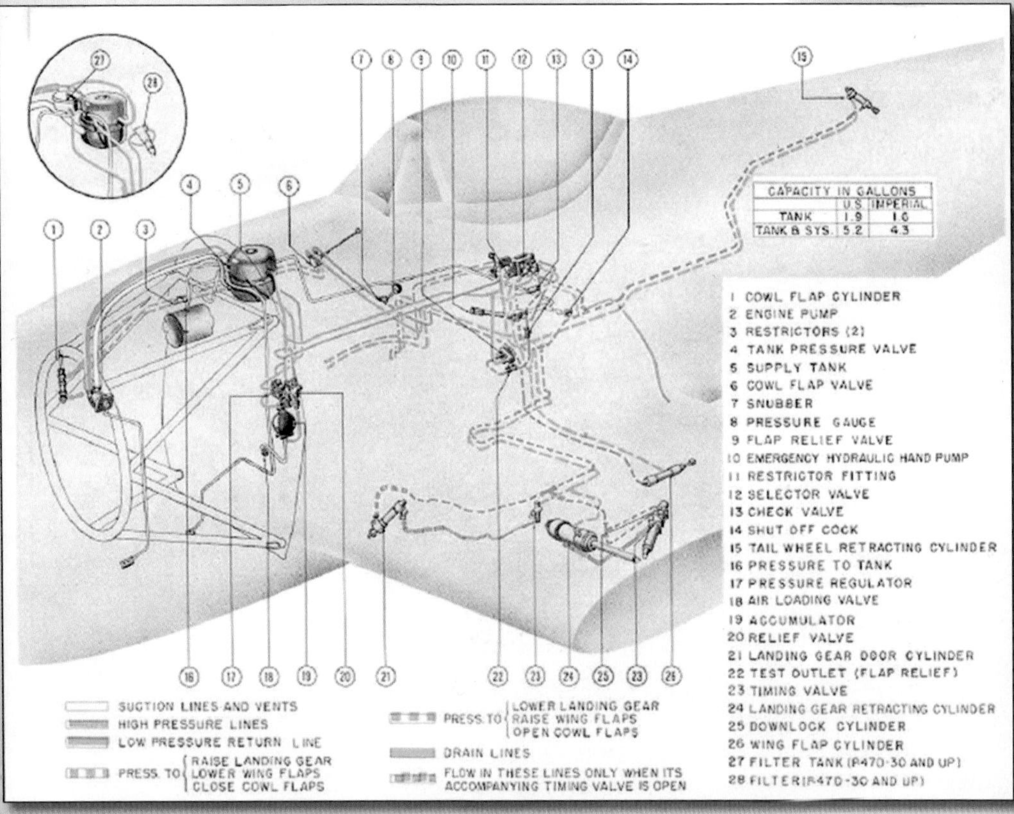

CAPACITY IN GALLONS
U.S.
IMPERIAL
TANK 1.9 1.6
TANK & SYS. 5.2 4.3
1 COWL FLAP CYLINDER
2 ENGINE PUMP
3 RESTRICTORS (2)
4 TANK PRESSURE VALVE
5 SUPPLY TANK
6 COWL FLAP VALVE
7 SNUBBER
8 PRESSURE GAUGE
9 FLAP RELIEF VALVE
10 EMERGENCY HYDRAULIC HAND PUMP
11 RESTRICTOR FITTING
12 SELECTOR VALVE
13 CHECK VALVE
14 SHUT OFF COCK
15 TAIL WHEEL RETRACTING CYLINDER
16 PRESSURE TO TANK
17 PRESSURE REGULATOR
18 AIR LOADING VALVE
19 ACCUMULATOR
20 RELIEF VALVE
21 LANDING GEAR DOOR CYLINDER
22 TEST OUTLET (FLAP RELIEF)
23 TIMING VALVE
24 LANDING GEAR RETRACTING CYLINDER
25 DOWNLOCK CYLINDER
26 WING FLAP CYLINDER
27 FILTER TANK (P47D-30 AND UP)
28 FILTER (P47D-30 AND UP)
SUCTION LINES AND VENTS
HIGH PRESSURE LINES
LOW PRESSURE RETURN LINE
PRESS. TO RAISE LANDING GEAR LOWER WING FLAPS CLOSE COWL FLAPS
PRESS. TO LOWER LANDING GEAR RAISE WING FLAPS OPEN COWL FLAPS
DRAIN LINES
FLOW IN THESE LINES ONLY WHEN ITS ACCOMPANYING TIMING VALVE IS OPEN

Right: The shapes of the outer doors can be seen in this view of the port main landing gear.

Below, right: Starboard outer doors. Note the small flap at the top of the upper outer door. This door closes an opening between the door and the wing when the gear is retracted.

Below: Inner view of the starboard main gear. There are 8 spokes on the wheel, but very often a flat disc was attached to cover the side of the wheel. Also the wheel with 6 spokes was commonly used during WWII.

(All photos R. Pęczkowski)

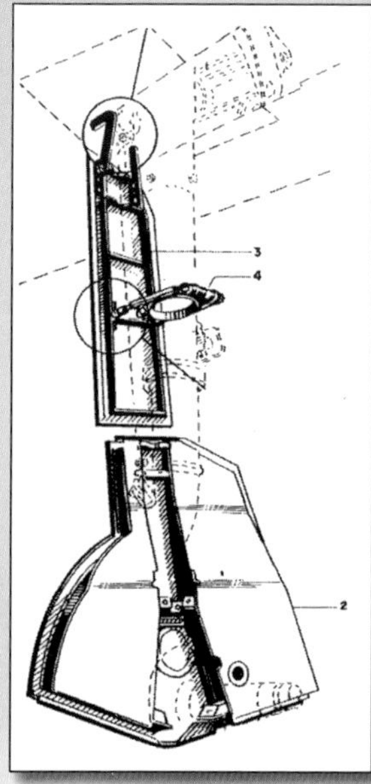

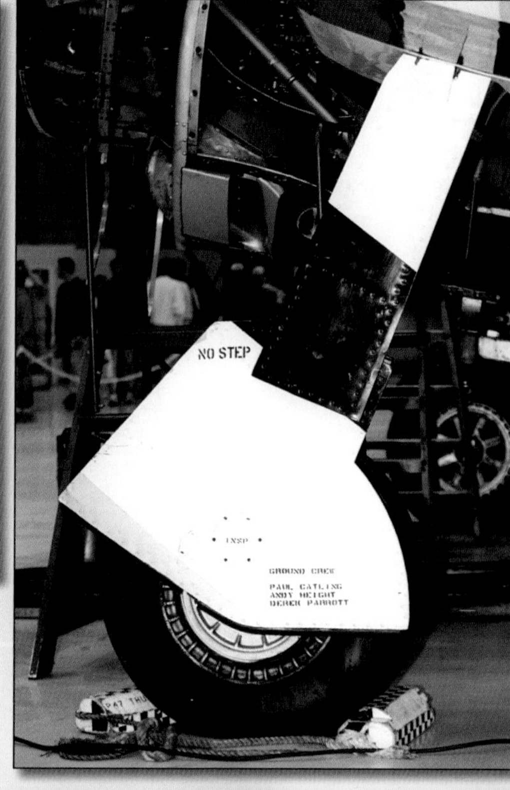

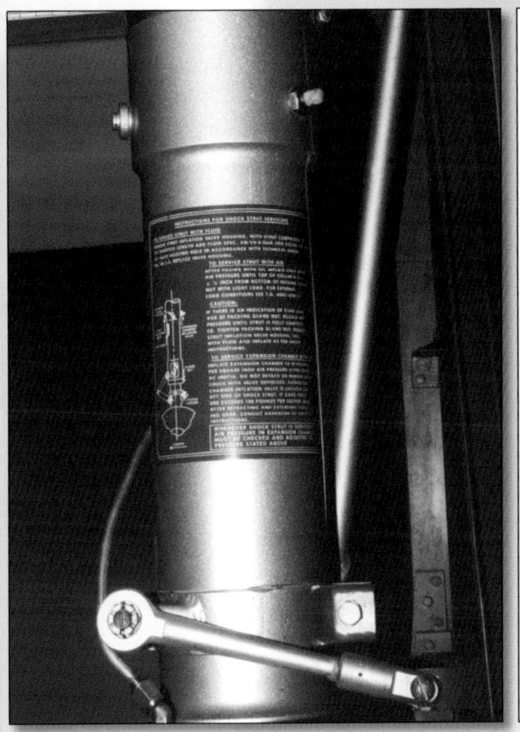

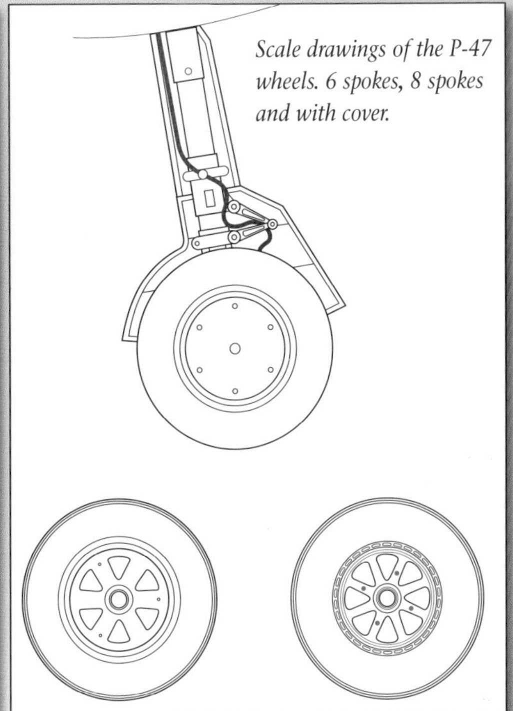

Scale drawings of the P-47 wheels. 6 spokes, 8 spokes and with cover.

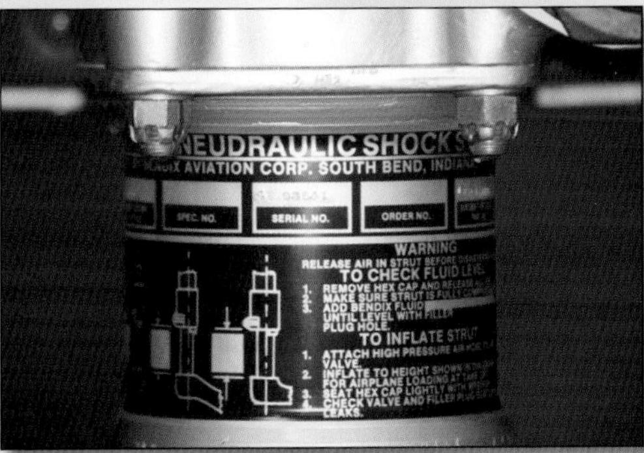

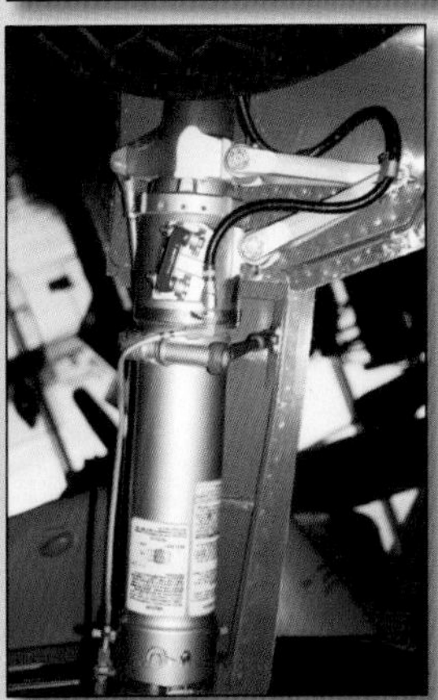

Four photos showing details of the main undercarriage leg. Photos:

(P. Wiśniewski)
(R. Pęczkowski)

Right and below: *Wheel with 6 spokes used during WWII.*

(P. Wiśniewski)

Right: *Wheel used mainly on P-47N, but retrofitted on P-47D used after the war.*

(P. Skulski)

Three photos showing P-47N undercarriage.
(P. Wiśniewski)

Photos of the wheel well details. The interior of the wells on the P-47 were painted Chromate Yellow on the Republic production lines. Chromate Green was used by Curtiss and sometimes applied in the field.

(P. Wiśniewski)

The next set of four photos showing wheel wells, but this time painted in silver.
Photos: (G. Papadimitriou via P. Skulski) (P. Wiśniewski)

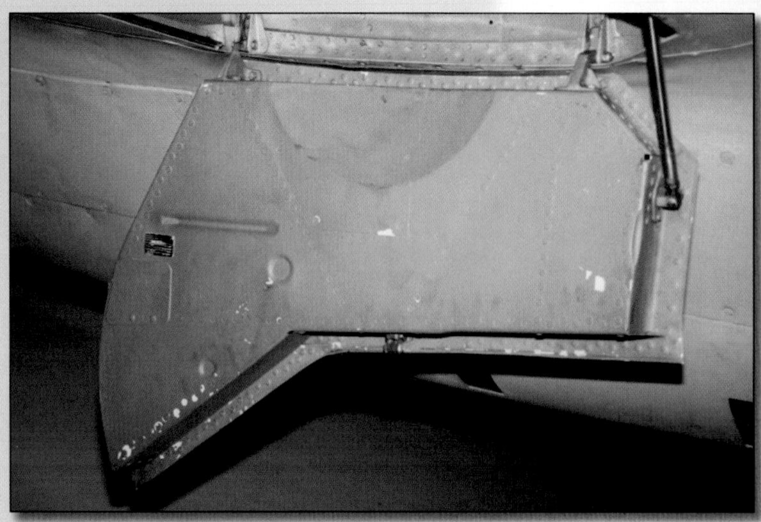

Above:
The hydraulic cylinder that actuated the main gear.

Right and below:
Three photos of the inner door of the main gear.
(P. Wiśniewski)
(via P. Skulski)

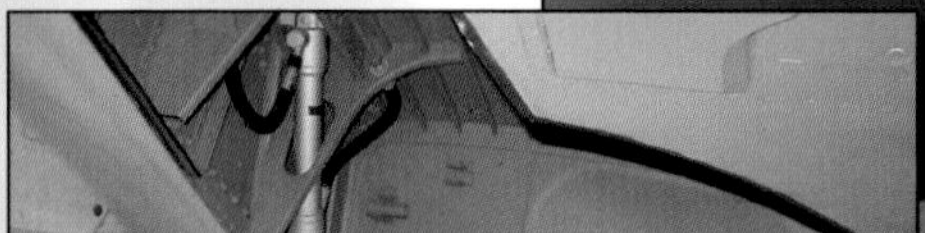

Above and above, right:
Two photos of the tail wheel with covers in open position.

Left:
Close up view of the tail wheel with the cover disc.

Bottom of the page:
Another view of the tail wheel.

(P. Wiśniewski),
(G. Papadimitriou via P. Skulski)

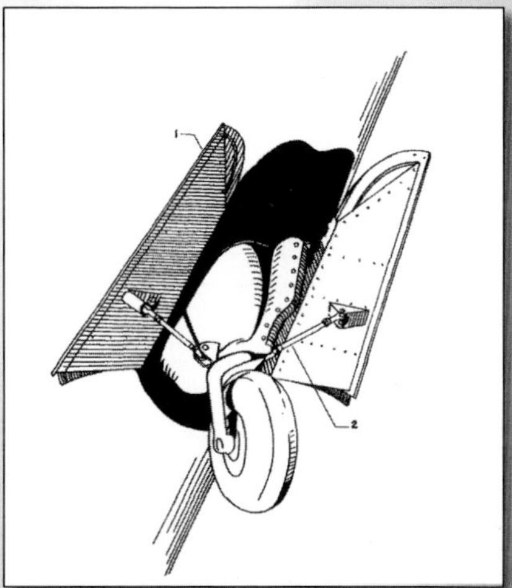

Two photos of the tail wheel well. The two arms which open and close the tail wheel doors are visible.
(P. Przymusiała)

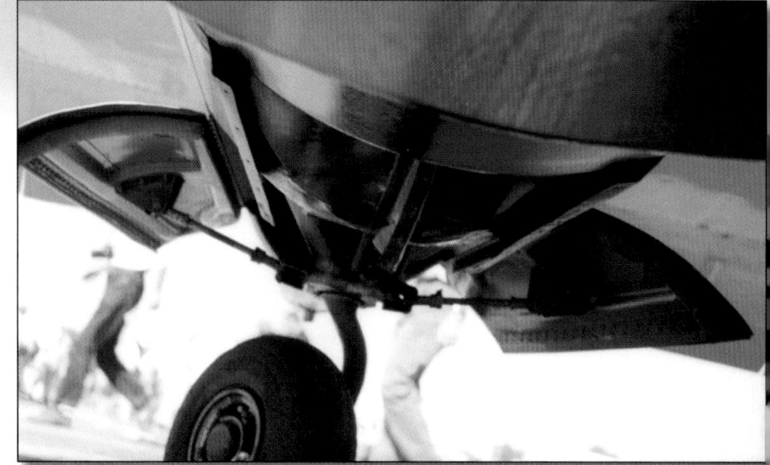

Below:
Tail wheel doors fully open, show the details of the tail gear mounting.
(R. Pęczkowski)

ARMAMENT

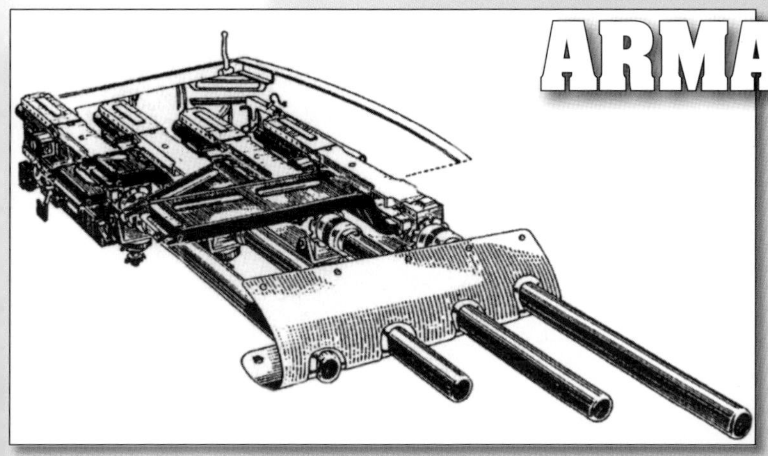

Drawing from Technical Manual showing the mounting of the .50 cal Browing M-2 machine guns in the port wing.

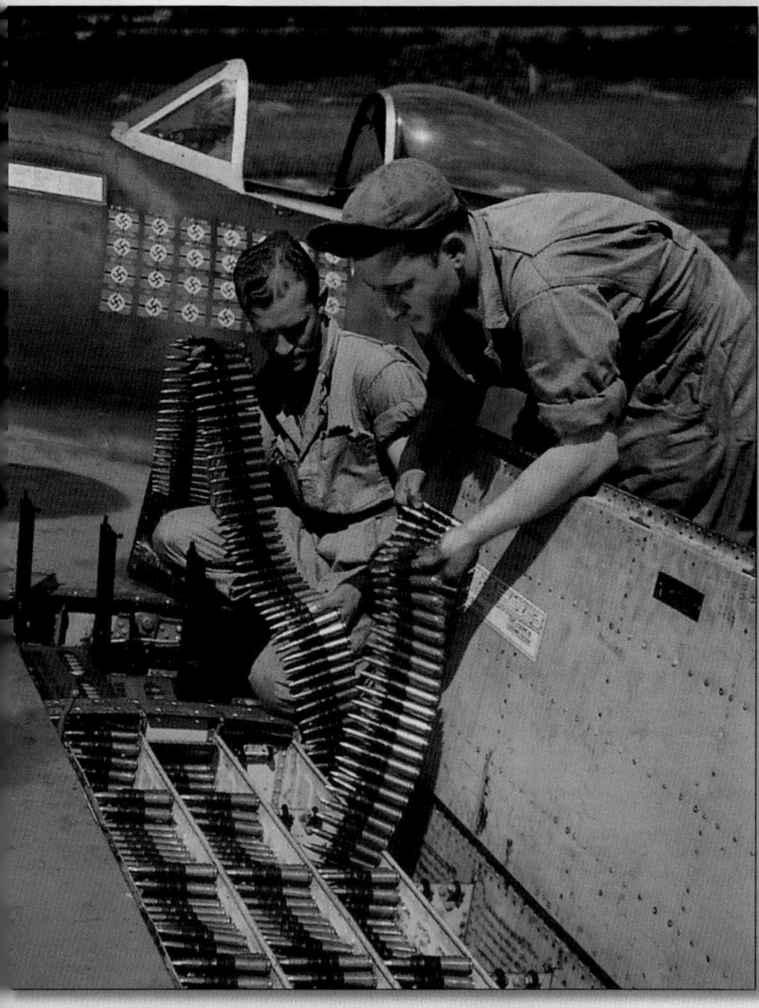

The well-known colour wartime photo of the F. Gabreski's P-47D. Armourers loading ammunition for the port guns. Republic painted the interior of the gun bays with Chromate Yellow and Curtiss in Chromate Green.
(US National Archives)

Original wartime photo showing starboard machine gun ammunition loading.
(US National Archives)

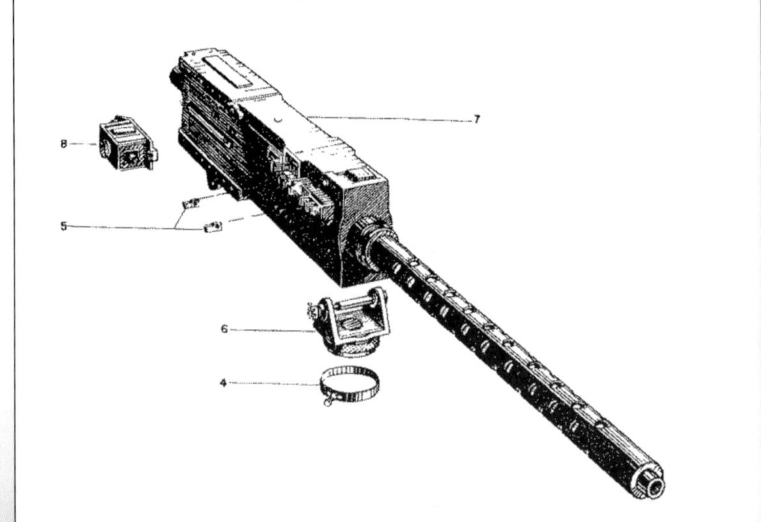

Drawing of 0.5 in. Browning M-2 machine gun assembly.
(Drawing from Maintenance Instructions)

Photo of the .50 calibre machine guns alignment in the leading edge of the port wing.
(R. Pęczkowski)

Cartridge ejection chutes of the machine guns under the port wing.
(R. Pęczkowski)

Interesting photo showing machine guns barrels and rocket rails. Bomb racks are also visible.
(Kenneth Kik)

Two photo showing machine gun rearming.

(US National Archives)

Photos of the 500lb. bomb on the wing pylon. This pylon was used on all bubbletop P-47 versions. (P. Wiśniewski)

Above: *Unidentified P-47D of the 353rd FG in "Thunderbomber" mode with 3 x 500 lb bombs. Note this was the same bomb-load as a Fairey Battle a light bomber!*

Bottom: *Two photos of bomb loading.*
(All photos US National Archives)

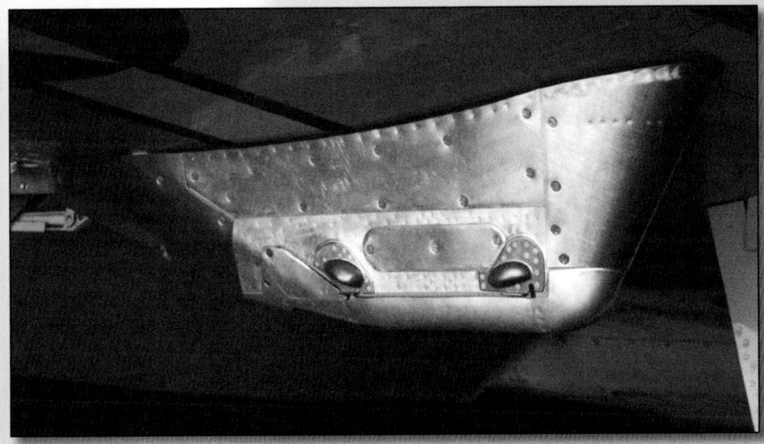

Two photos of the under-wing pylons without bracing but with special covers to reduce drag when not carrying ordnance.
(Both photos P. Wiśniewski)

Detail shot of the gun barrels and rocket rails.
In the cockpit is Robert Martin of 397th FS.
(Kenneth Kik)

Two photos of the M26 cluster bombs used on Thunderbolts.
(P. Wiśniewski)

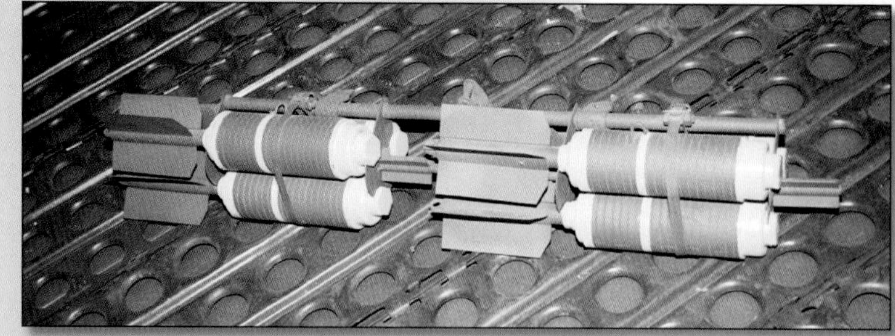

Below: *M26 cluster bomb on the P-47D underwing pylon.*
(US National Archives)

Two photos of P-47Ds with Bazzooka rocket launchers under the wing.
(US National Archives)

Top: Two photos of rocket rails on P-47D preserved in Belgrad.
Photos
***Bottom:** Underwing pylon without its fairing.*
(G. Papadimitriou via. P. Skulski)
(M. Orlog)

Opposite page top:
Bazooka rocket loading. Note 500 lb bomb on the underwing pylon.
(Stratus coll.)

Opposite page bottom:
P-47D of 78th FG with 20 mm guns mounted on the wing pylons. Duxford, October 1944.
(US National Archives)

P-47D somewhere in the Pacific. Note the P-38 style 150 gal. underwing fuel tanks.
(US National Archives)

Bottom: *P-47D loaded with two 500lb bombs and 75 gal drop tank under fuselage.*
(J. Sterling)

F-47D-30-RA, No. 850 of 10 Esquadron de Caza, Colombian Air Force, (Fuerza Aerea Colombiana – FAC). Natural metal overall, with black anti glare panel and red cowling and spinner.

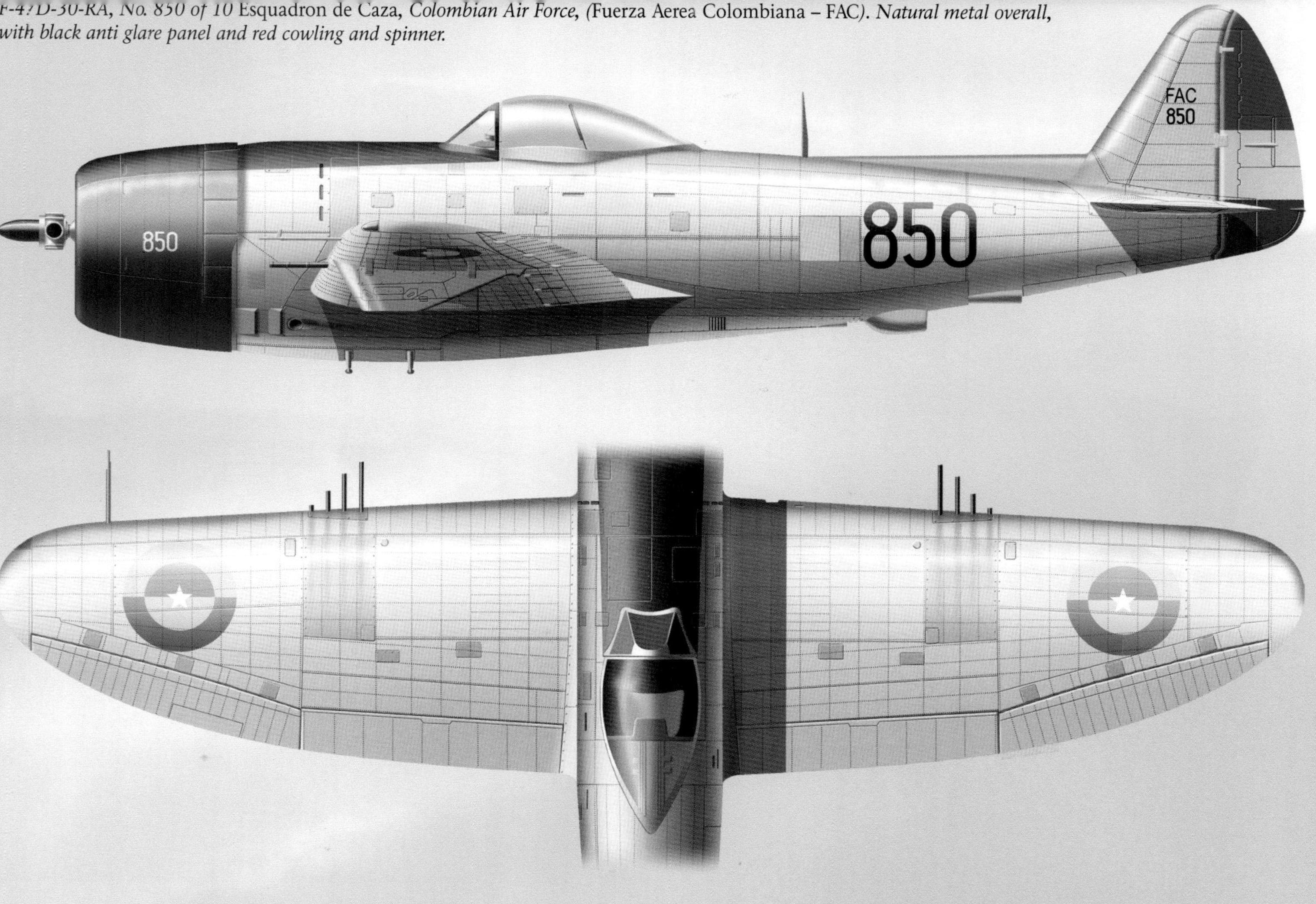

Famous colour photo of Lt. Col. F. S. Gabreski in his P-47D. (US National Archives)

Gabreski and his crew. S/Sgt. R.H. Safford – Crew chief, Cpl. Felix Schacki – Asst. Crew chief, Sgt. Joe DiFranza – armourer, Lt. Col. F. Gabreski P-47D-25 s/n 42-26418 of the 56th FG, 61st FS, July 1944.

***Right:** The personal reminiscences of both Gabreski and his fitter indicate that the P-47 was painted overall in RAF colours, including Medium Sea Grey undersides. However, photos indicate that the black ETO bands, painted on to natural metal airframes, remained on Gabreski's P-47 under the tailplanes at least. As it seems highly unlikely that the ETO bands were repainted on camouflaged surfaces, one can deduce that the undersides of the tailplanes, at least, remained unpainted. No clear photographic evidence is available to us to deduce the precise underside colours of the rest of this particular aircraft - other 56th FG P-47s with RAF camouflaged topsides retained their NM undersides.*

(P. Wiśniewski coll.)

Two photos of P-47D-25-RE, serial 42-26418 "HV-A". Flying this machine F. S. Gabreski made a forced landing on 20.07.1944 and became a POW.

(T. J. Kopański coll.)

TEMCO F-47D-30-RA, *then converted to D-40 standard, serial 45-49219, No. 750 of Grupo II, Chilean Air Force.* (Fuerza Aerea de Chile). *Delivered on 18/7/53. Natural metal overall. Now at Santiago's Aeronautical Museum*

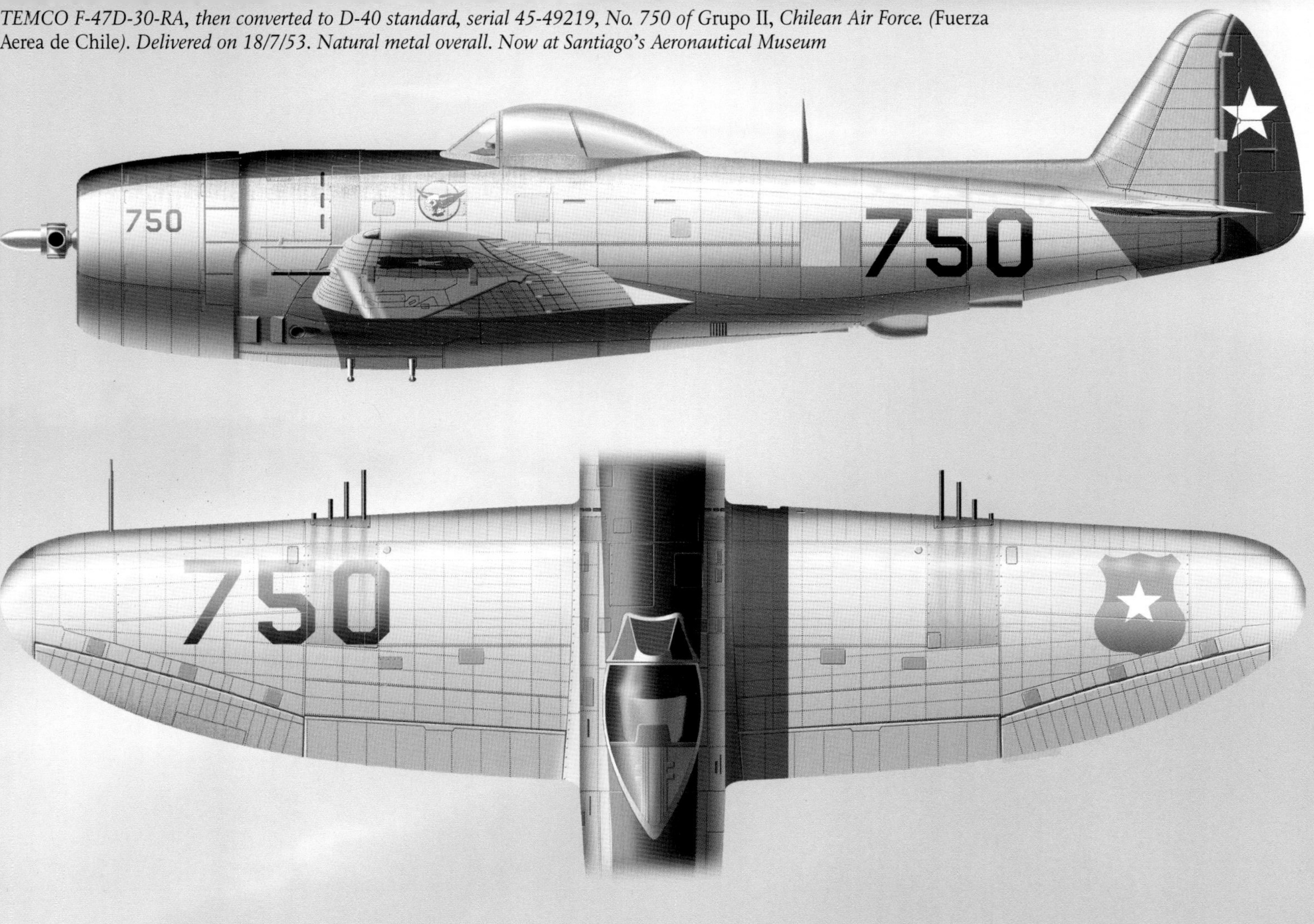

Refuelling P-47D, A6 of of 1° GavCa, 350th Brazilian AF.
(US National Archives)

Wartime colour photo of Brazilian P-47D.
(US National Archives)

P-47 D-25-RE, *serial 42-26762 "C1", of 1° GavCa, 350th FG, Brazilian AF (Forca Aerea Brasileira – FAB) as a part of 12 AF. Personal aircraft of Capt. Fortunato Camara de Oliveira. Olive Drab and Neutral Grey. Propeller hub is natural metal.*

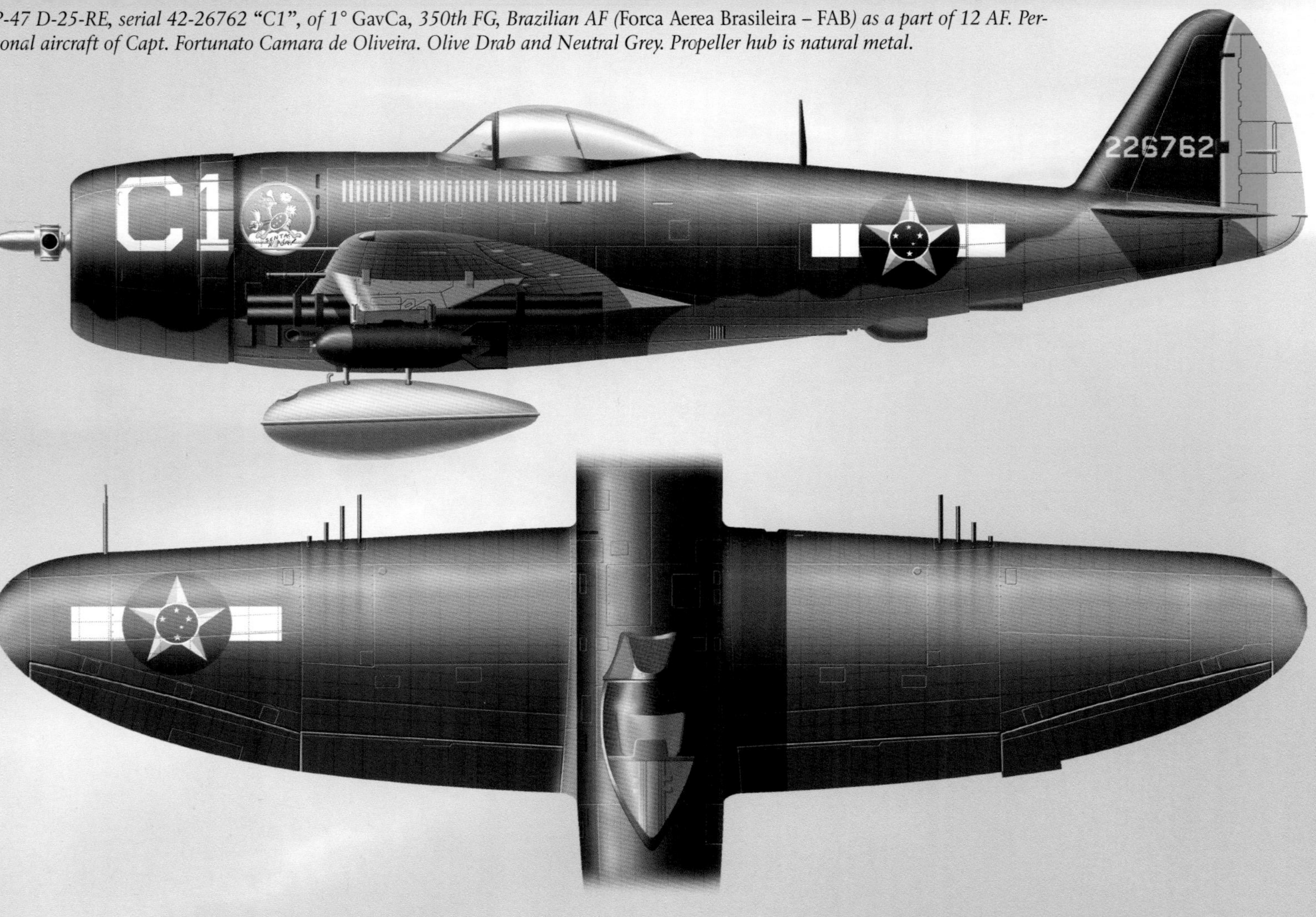

Engine cowling with personal emblem "Rough and Ready" of William Garry.
P-47D-28-RE, s/n 44-20268, A7-G of 368th FG, 395th FS.

(Kenneth Kik)

Colour profile see opposite page, left.

Two photos of P-47D-28-RE, s/n 44-20089, C2-Q, "Leaky Joe 5" of 368th FG, 396th FS. Personal aircraft of Irving Ostuw.
In the bottom photo his Thunderbolt has German occupation stripes added to the rear fuselage.

(Kenneth Kik)

Colour profile see opposite page, right.

420268
A7 G
420089
C2 Q

Three photos of P-47D-30-RE, s/n 44-20456 D3-V, "Lizzy" of 368th FG, 397th FS. Personal aircraft of Les Leavoy. Note that aircraft has P-47N style dorsal fillet. Colour profile see opposite page.

(Kenneth Kik)

D3
V
420456

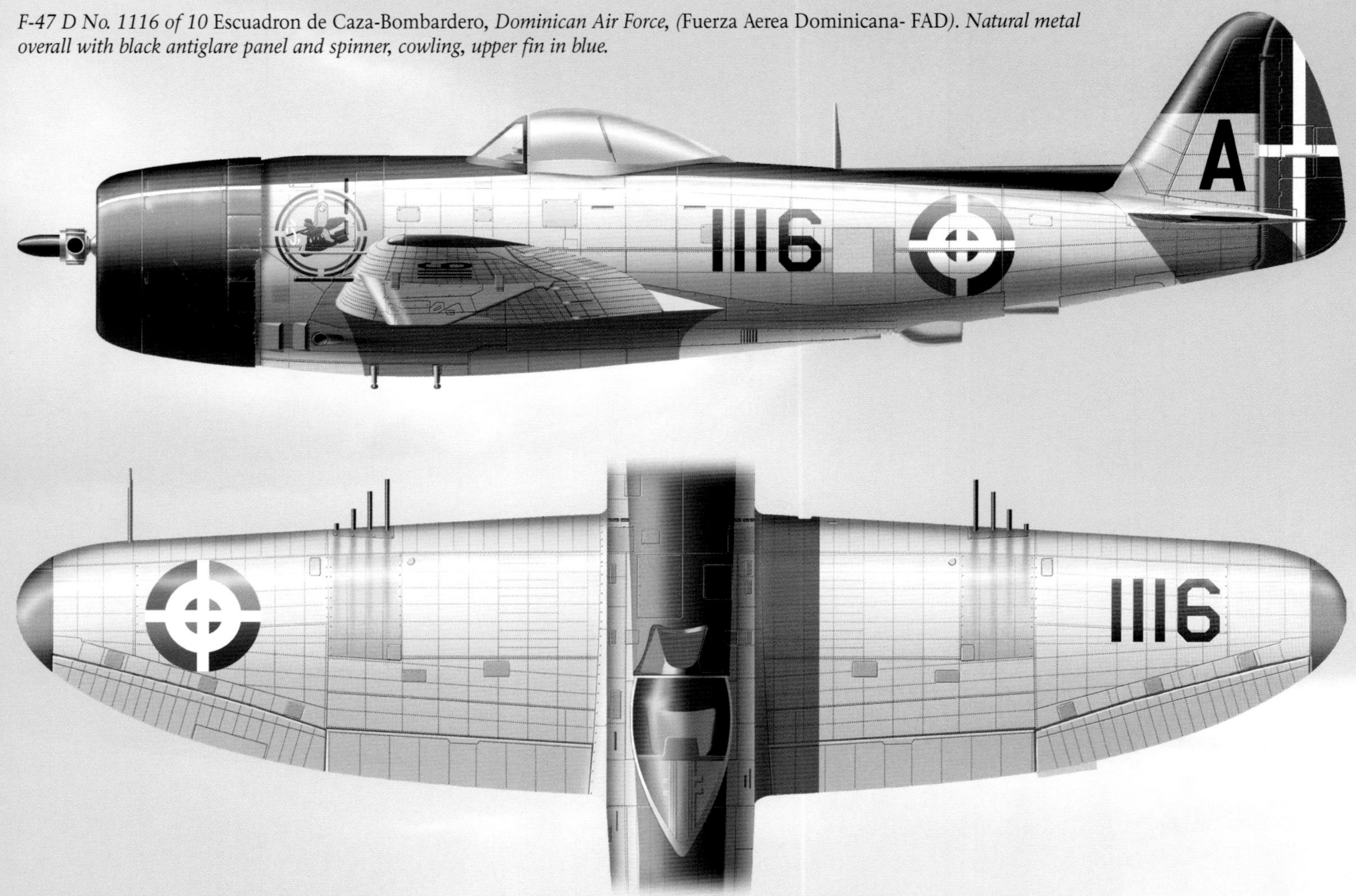

F-47 D No. 1116 of 10 Escuadron de Caza-Bombardero, *Dominican Air Force, (*Fuerza Aerea Dominicana- FAD*). Natural metal overall with black antiglare panel and spinner, cowling, upper fin in blue.*

F-47 D No. 1125 *of 10* Escuadron de Caza-Bombardero, *Dominican Air Force*, (Fuerza Aerea Dominicana- FAD). *Natural metal overall, black top of the fuselage with white trim. Red cowling and fuselage band with black trim..*

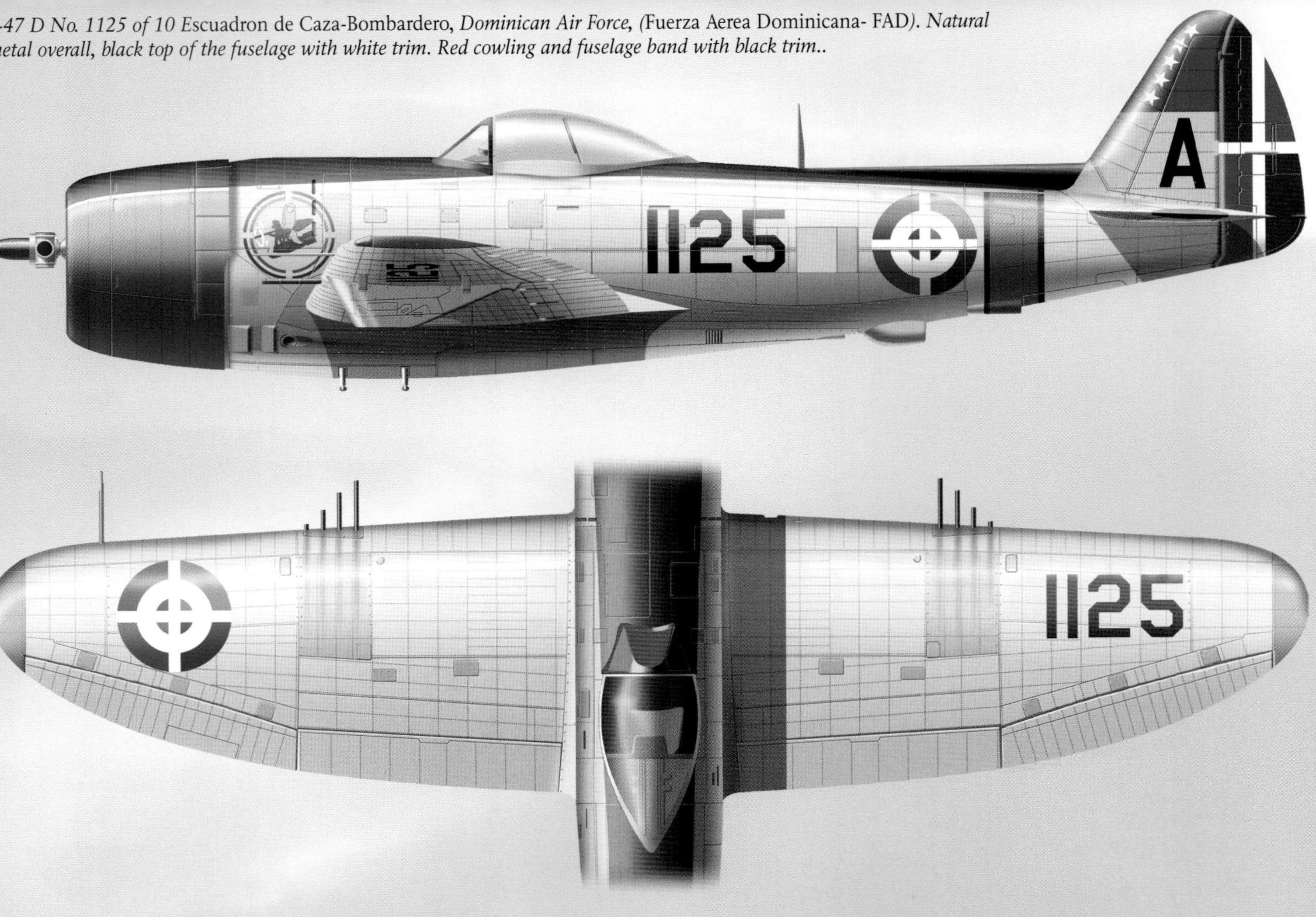

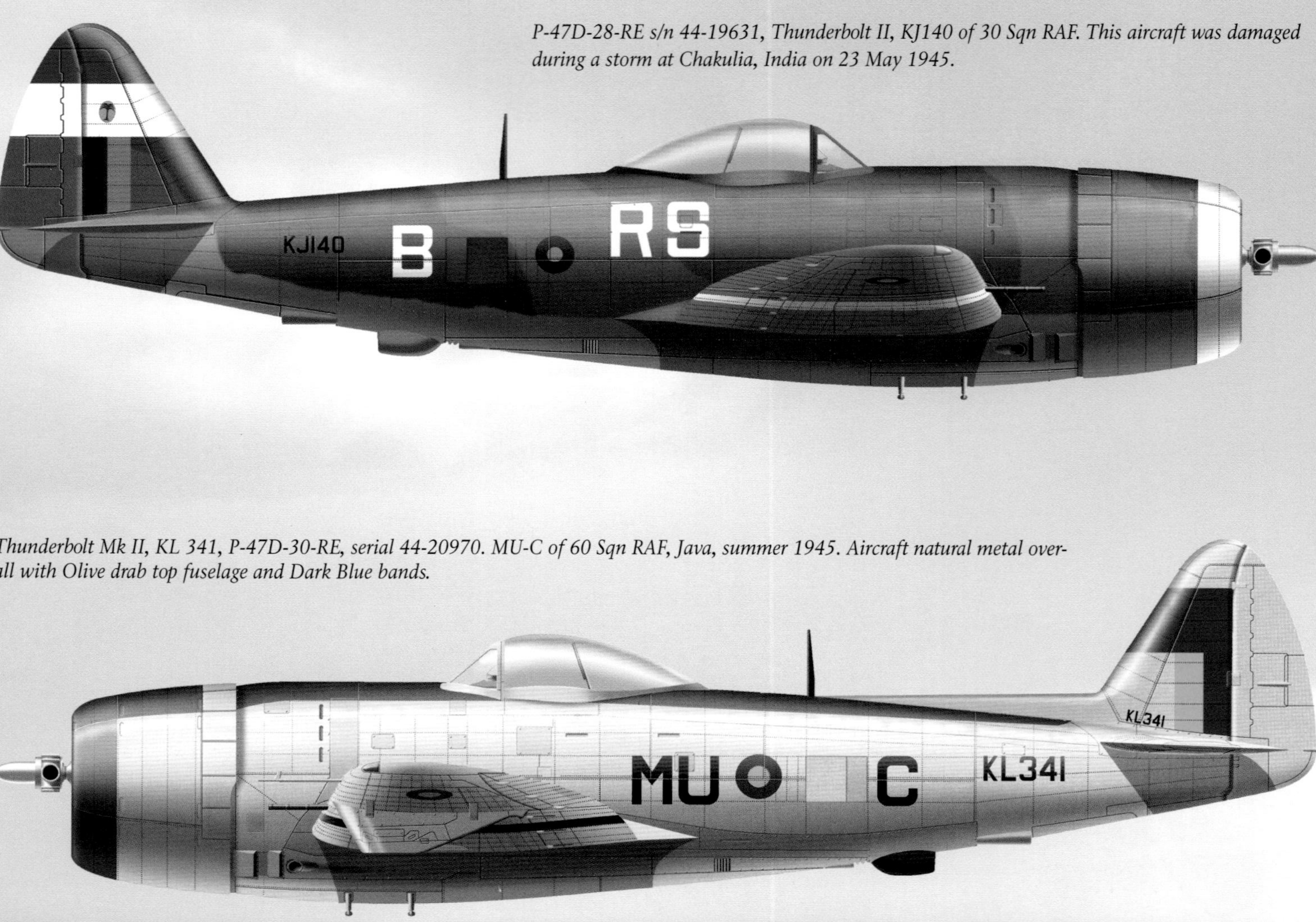

P-47D-28-RE s/n 44-19631, Thunderbolt II, KJ140 of 30 Sqn RAF. This aircraft was damaged during a storm at Chakulia, India on 23 May 1945.

Thunderbolt Mk II, KL 341, P-47D-30-RE, serial 44-20970. MU-C of 60 Sqn RAF, Java, summer 1945. Aircraft natural metal overall with Olive drab top fuselage and Dark Blue bands.

P-47D-30-RE, MM4631, '5-11' of 5° Stormo, *Italian Air Force, early 1950s.*

P-47D-30-RA, serial 44-33397 of GC II/5, escadrille "Lafayette", *Free French Air Force, 1944. Natural metal overall.*

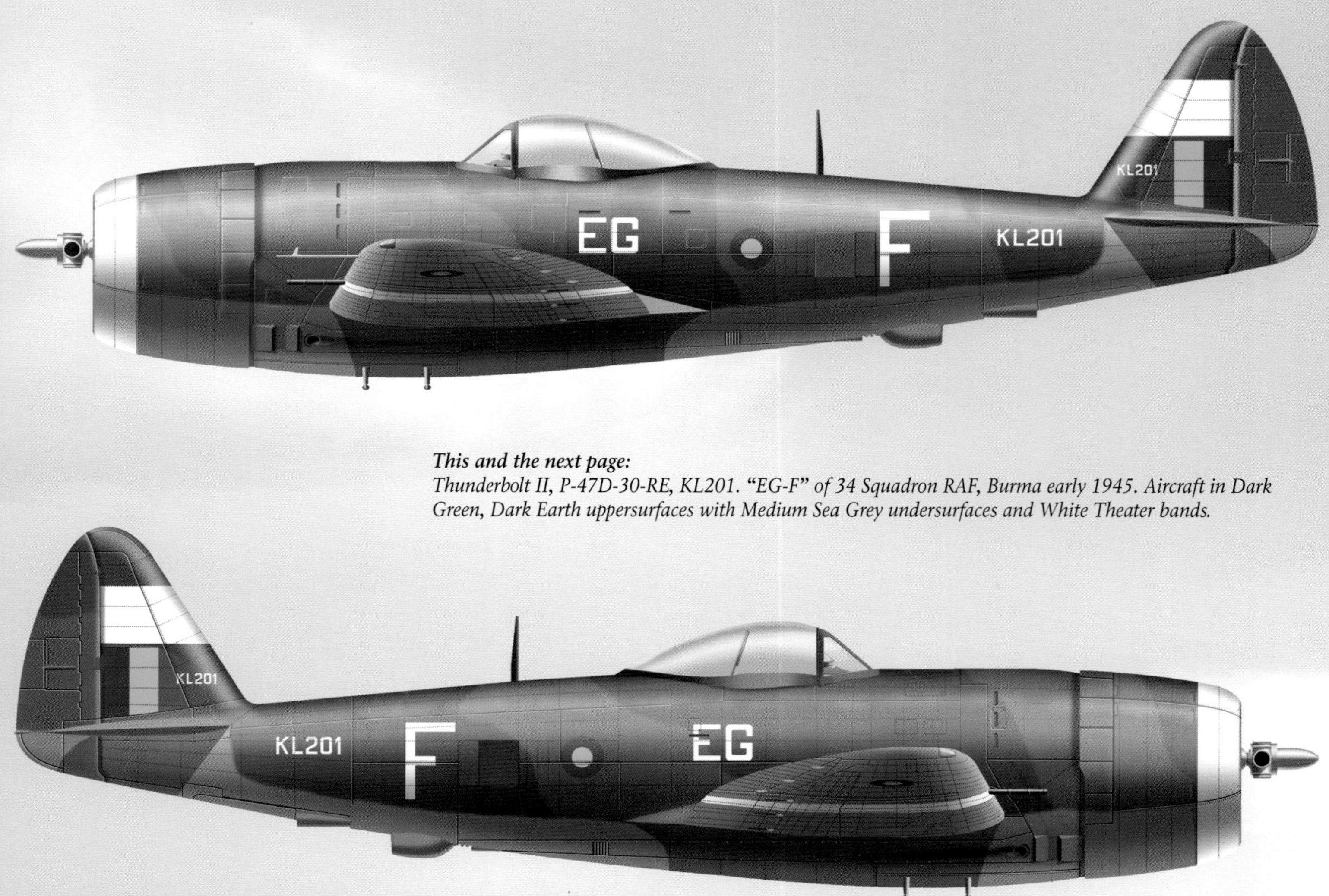

This and the next page:
Thunderbolt II, P-47D-30-RE, KL201. "EG-F" of 34 Squadron RAF, Burma early 1945. Aircraft in Dark Green, Dark Earth uppersurfaces with Medium Sea Grey undersurfaces and White Theater bands.

P-47D-28-RE, serial 44-20050 of GC I/4, Free French Air Force, 1945. Personal Aircraft of P. Muselli. Olive Drab and Neutral Grey.

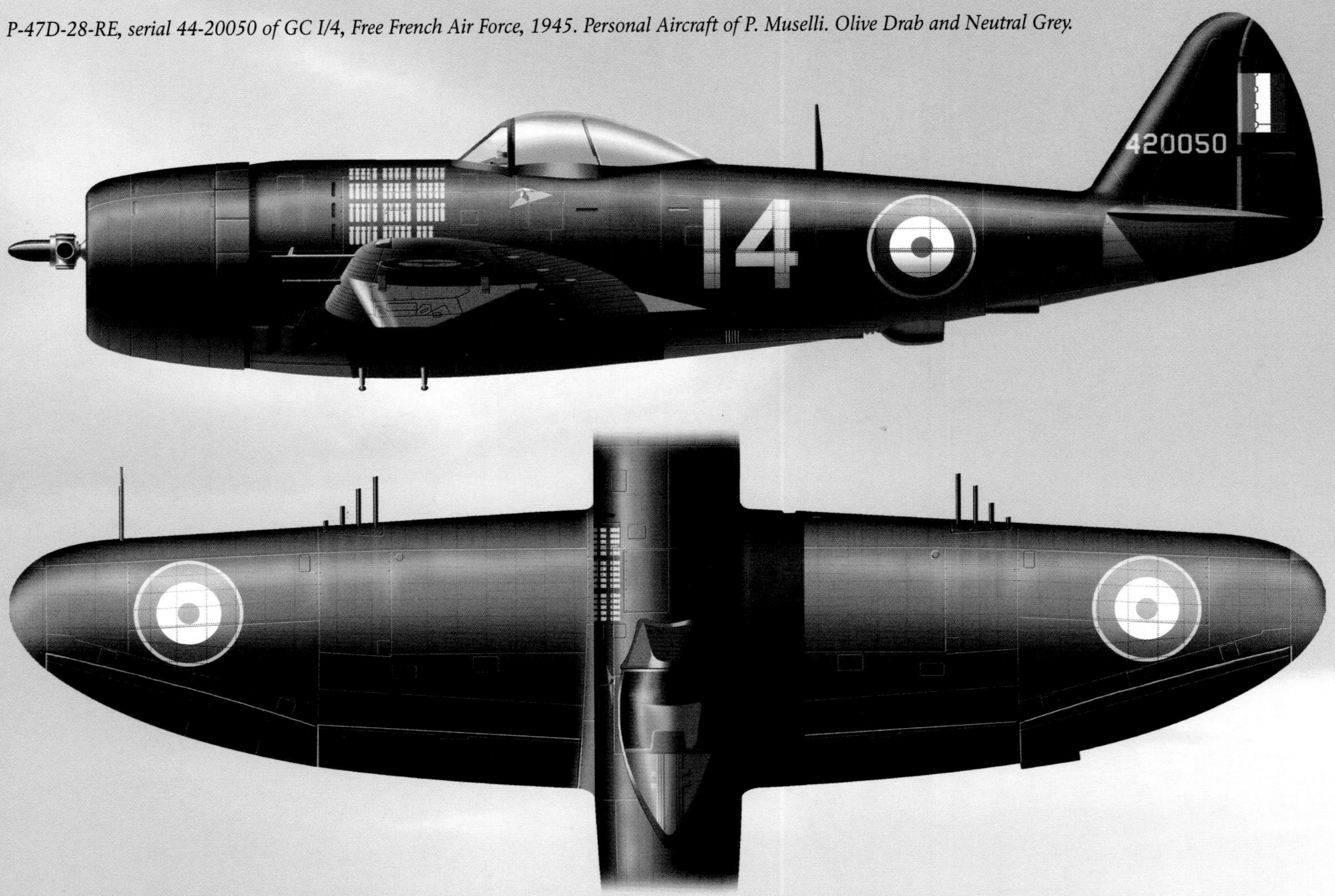

P-47D-30-RA, serial 44-33478, "256" of Imperial Iranian Air Force. Aircraft natural metal overall with Olive Drab fuselage top and green cowling.

F-47D No. 464 of 10 Esquadron de Caza-Bombardero, *Cuban Air Force, (*Fuerza Aerea Ejercitio de Cuba –FEAC*). Natural metal overall.*

F-47D No. 476 of 10 Esquadron de Caza-Bombardero, *Cuban Air Force* (Fuerza Aerea Ejercitio de Cuba –FEAC), 1957-58. *Upper surfaces khaki and black, lower surfaces grey. Aircraft was repainted in Cuba.*

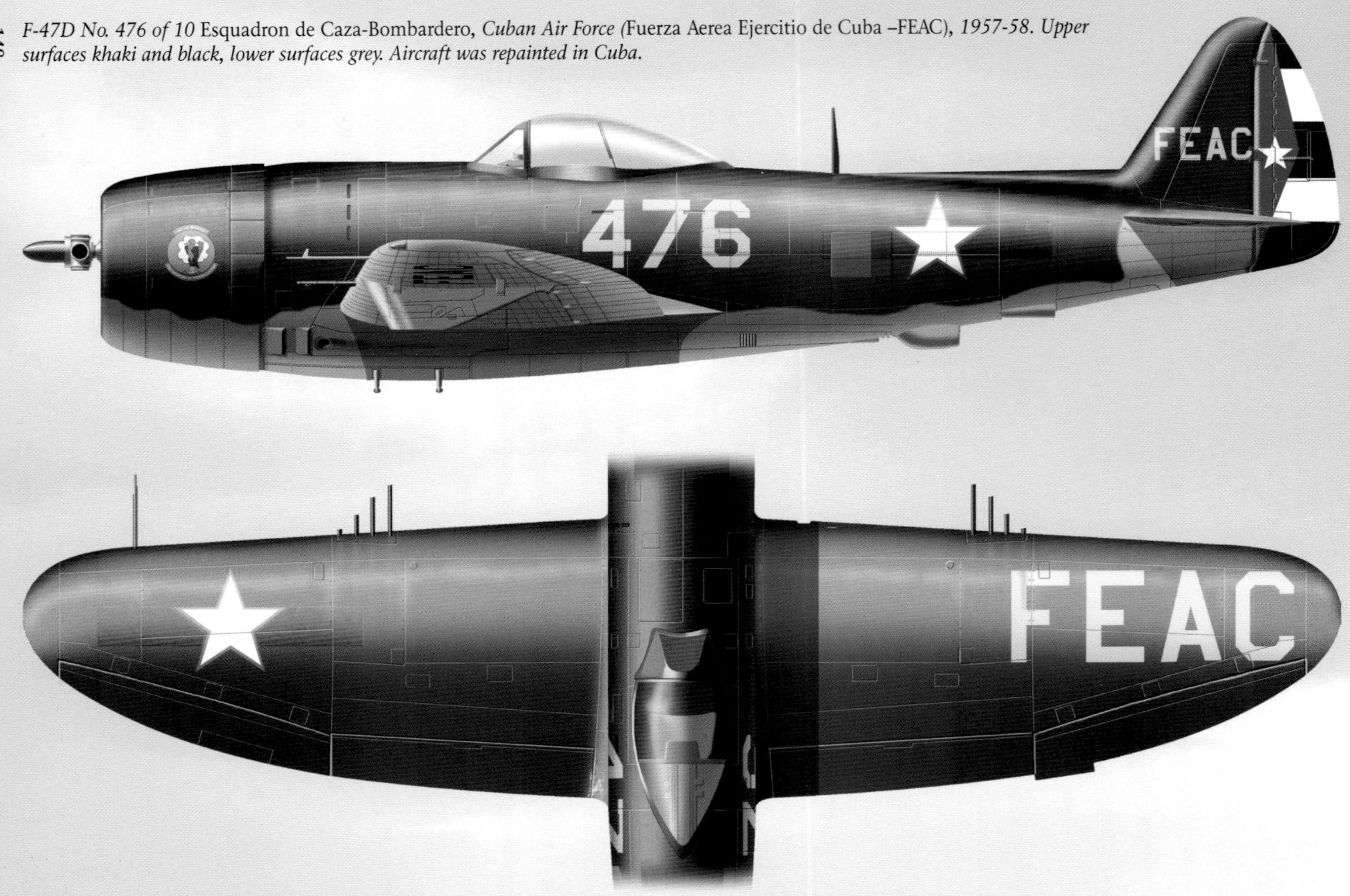

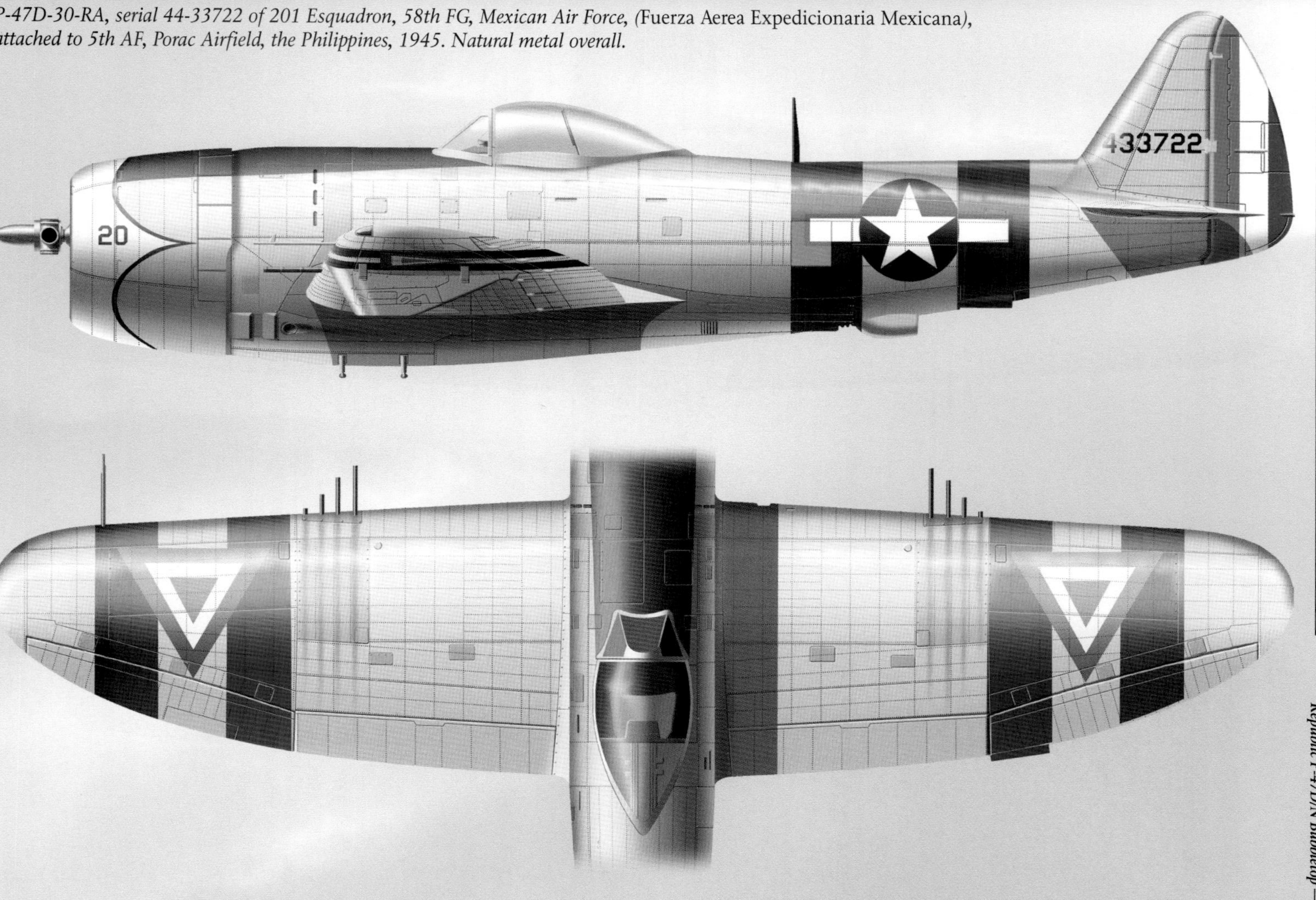

P-47D-30-RA, serial 44-33722 of 201 Esquadron, 58th FG, Mexican Air Force, (Fuerza Aerea Expedicionaria Mexicana), attached to 5th AF, Porac Airfield, the Philippines, 1945. Natural metal overall.

F-47D, PZT-1011 of 201 Esquadron, *Mexican Air Force,* (Fuerza Aerea Mexicana- FAM), 1959. *Olive Drab overall.*

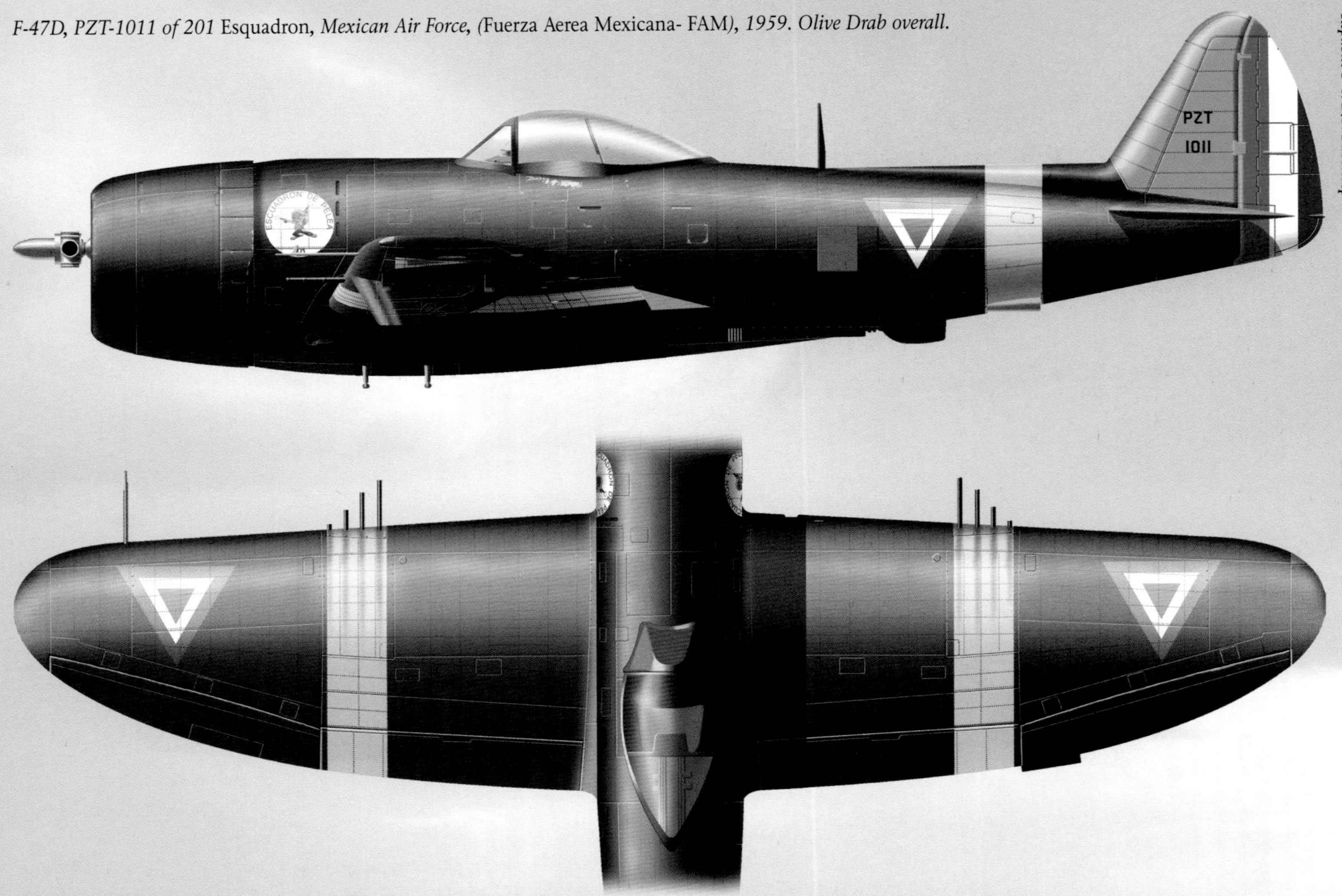

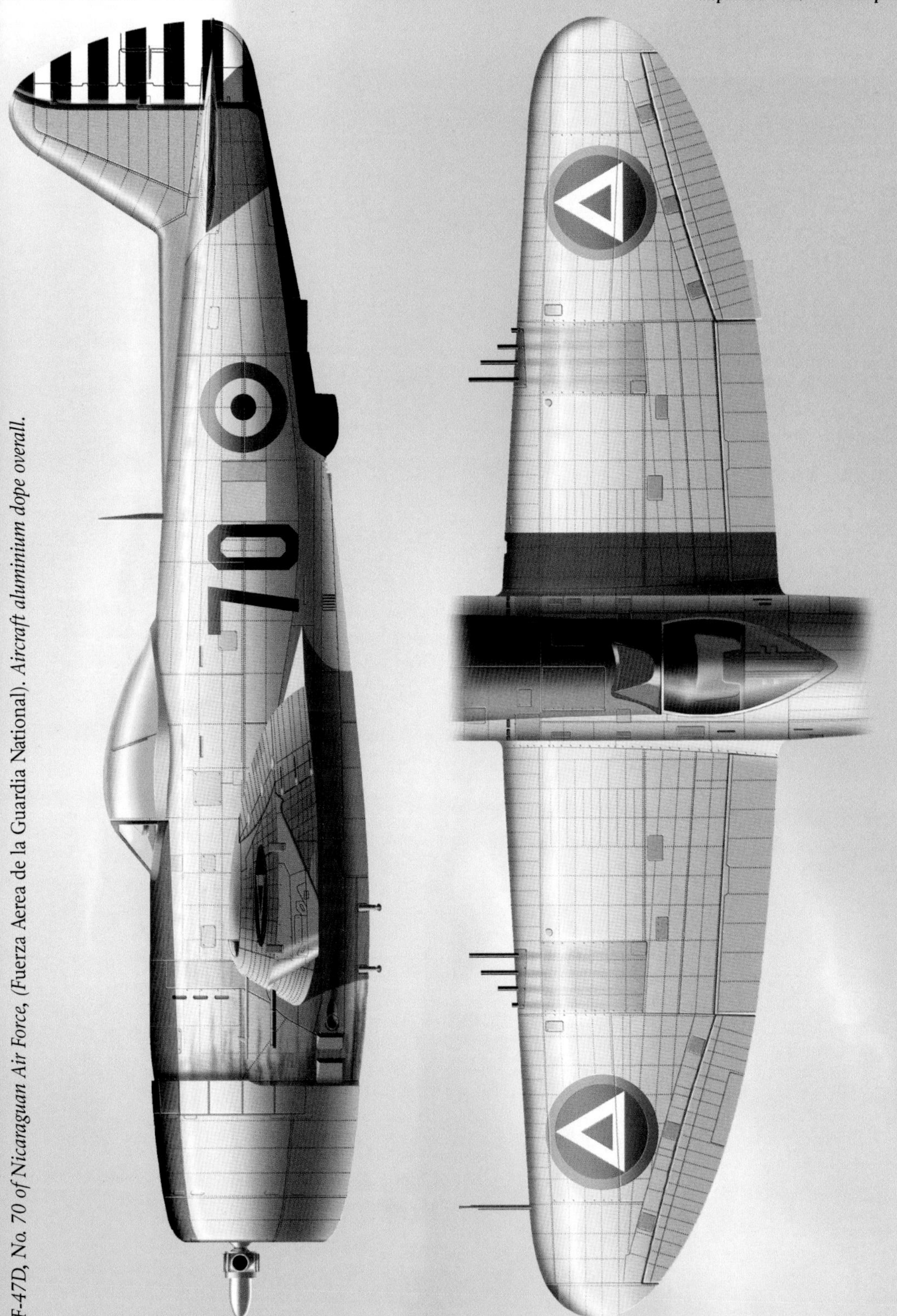

F-47D, No. 70 of *Nicaraguan Air Force*, (Fuerza Aerea de la Guardia National). *Aircraft aluminium dope overall.*

TEMCO *refurbished* TF-47D-40-RA, *serial* 45-49181, *No.* 115 *of Peruvian Air Force* (Fuerza Aerea del Peru – FAP). *Aircraft aluminium dope overall.*

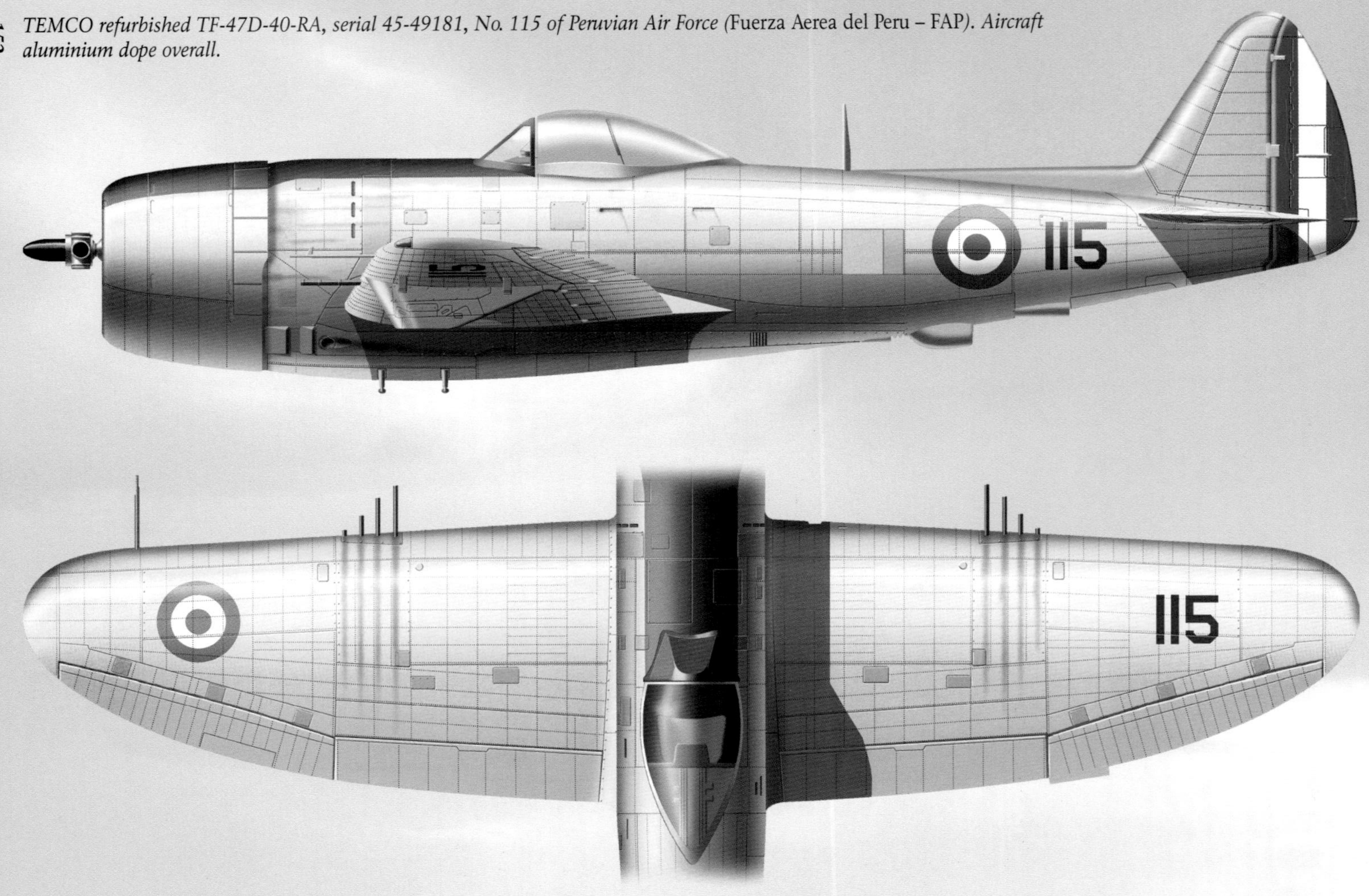

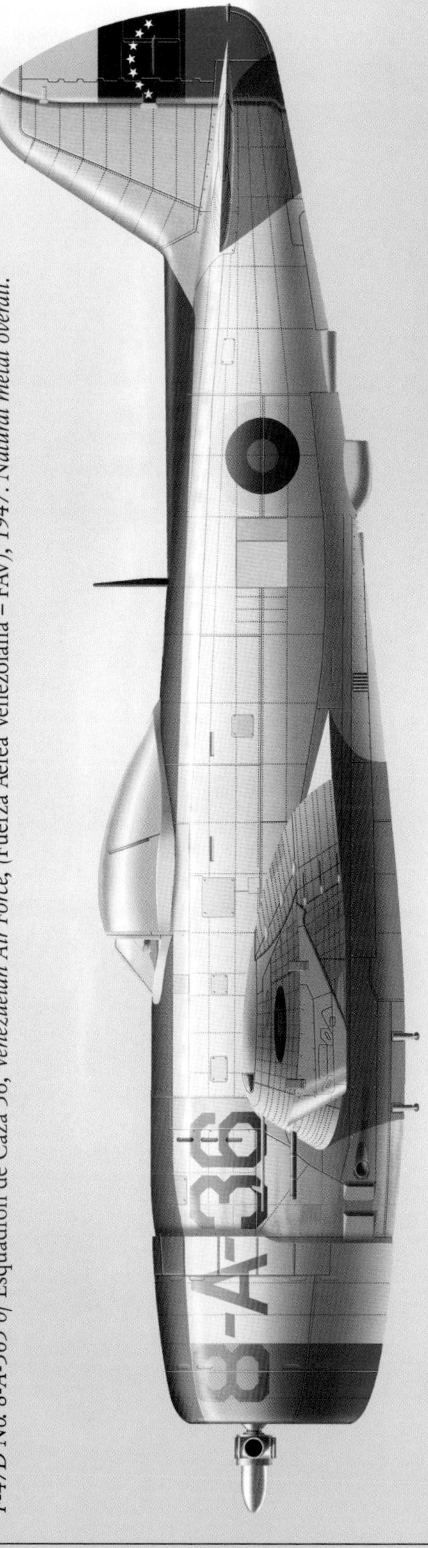

F-47D No. 8-A-365 of Esquadron de Caza 36, *Venezuelan Air Force*, (Fuerza Aerea Venezolana – FAV), 1947. *Natural metal overall.*

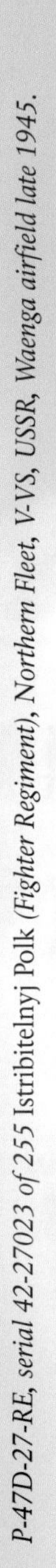

P-47D-27-RE, *serial 42-27023 of* 255 Istribitelnyj Polk *(Fighter Regiment), Northern Fleet, V-VS, USSR, Waenga airfield late 1945.*

P-47D-30-RA, *serial* 44-33712, "TC-21" *of the Turkish Air Force. Now preserved at Turkish Air Force Museum, Istanbul. Natural metal overall.*

P-47D *(probably D-30)*, No. "411" *of* 100 Esquadron, 1000 Ala de Caza-Bombarderro, *Ecuadorian Air Force*, (La Fuerza Aerea Ecuatariana). *Natural metal overall with Olive Drab top fuselage and red engine cowl.*

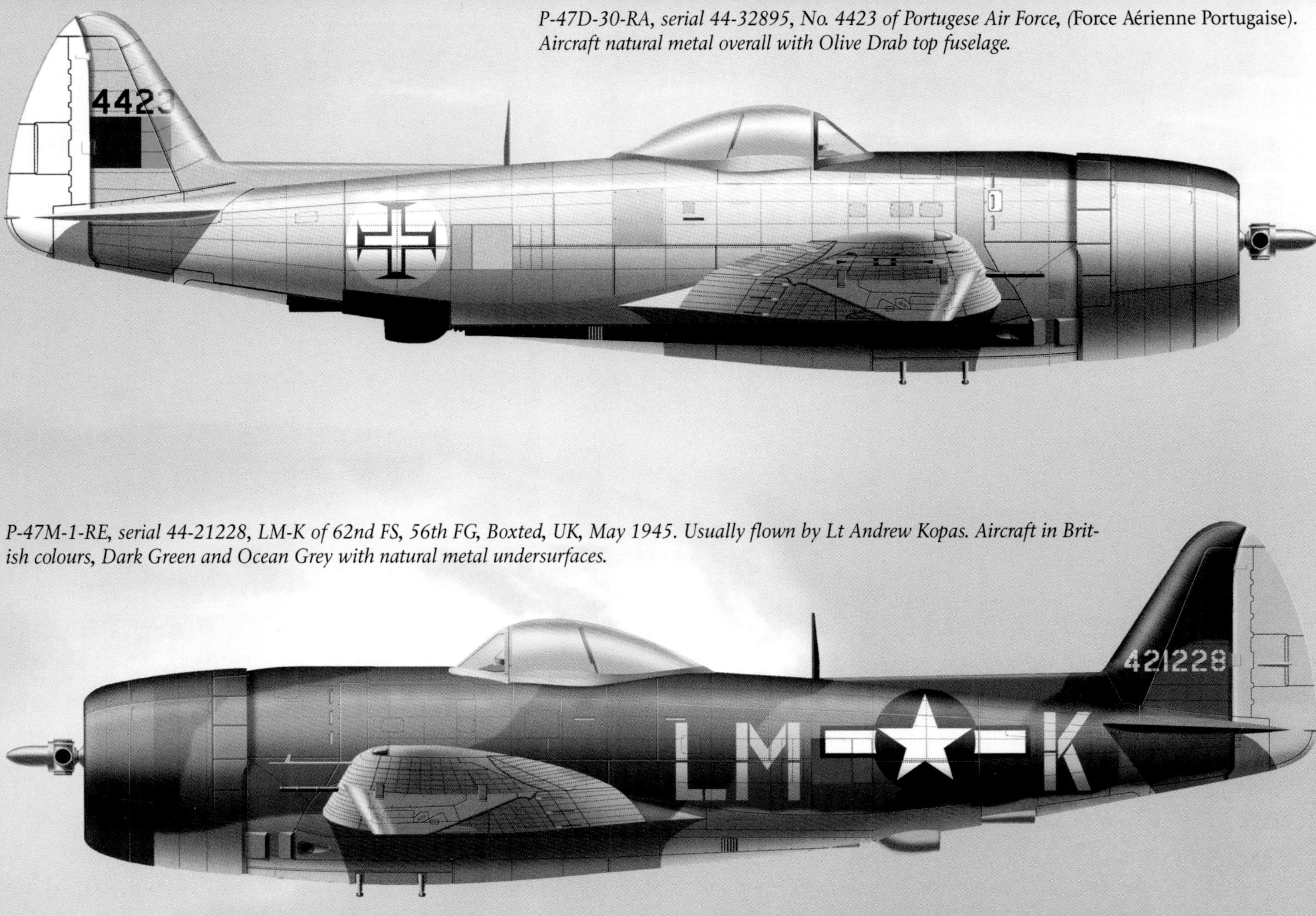

P-47D-30-RA, *serial 44-32895, No. 4423 of Portugese Air Force,* (Force Aérienne Portugaise). *Aircraft natural metal overall with Olive Drab top fuselage.*

P-47M-1-RE, *serial 44-21228, LM-K of 62nd FS, 56th FG, Boxted, UK, May 1945. Usually flown by Lt Andrew Kopas. Aircraft in British colours, Dark Green and Ocean Grey with natural metal undersurfaces.*

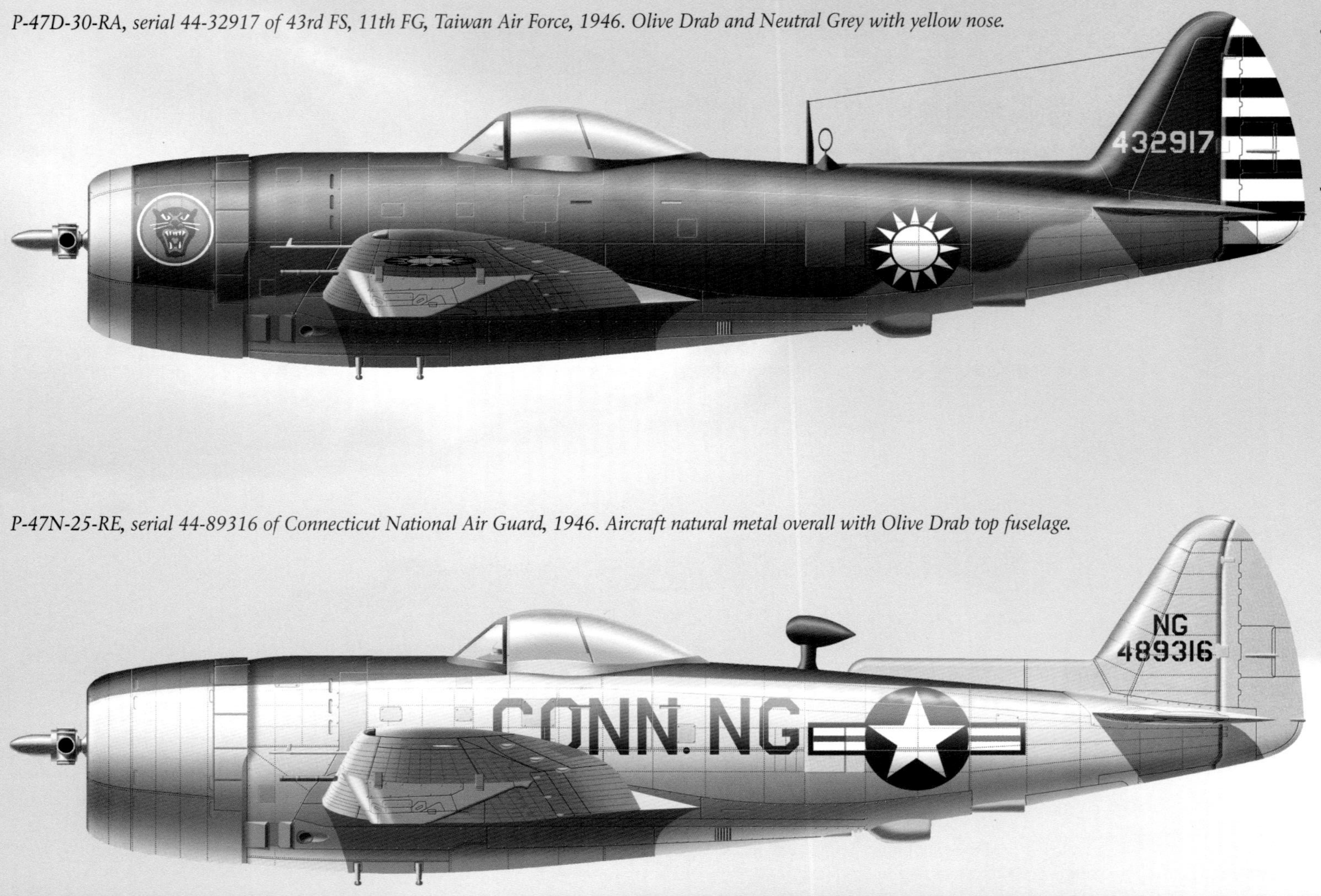

P-47D-30-RA, serial 44-32917 of 43rd FS, 11th FG, Taiwan Air Force, 1946. Olive Drab and Neutral Grey with yellow nose.

P-47N-25-RE, serial 44-89316 of Connecticut National Air Guard, 1946. Aircraft natural metal overall with Olive Drab top fuselage.

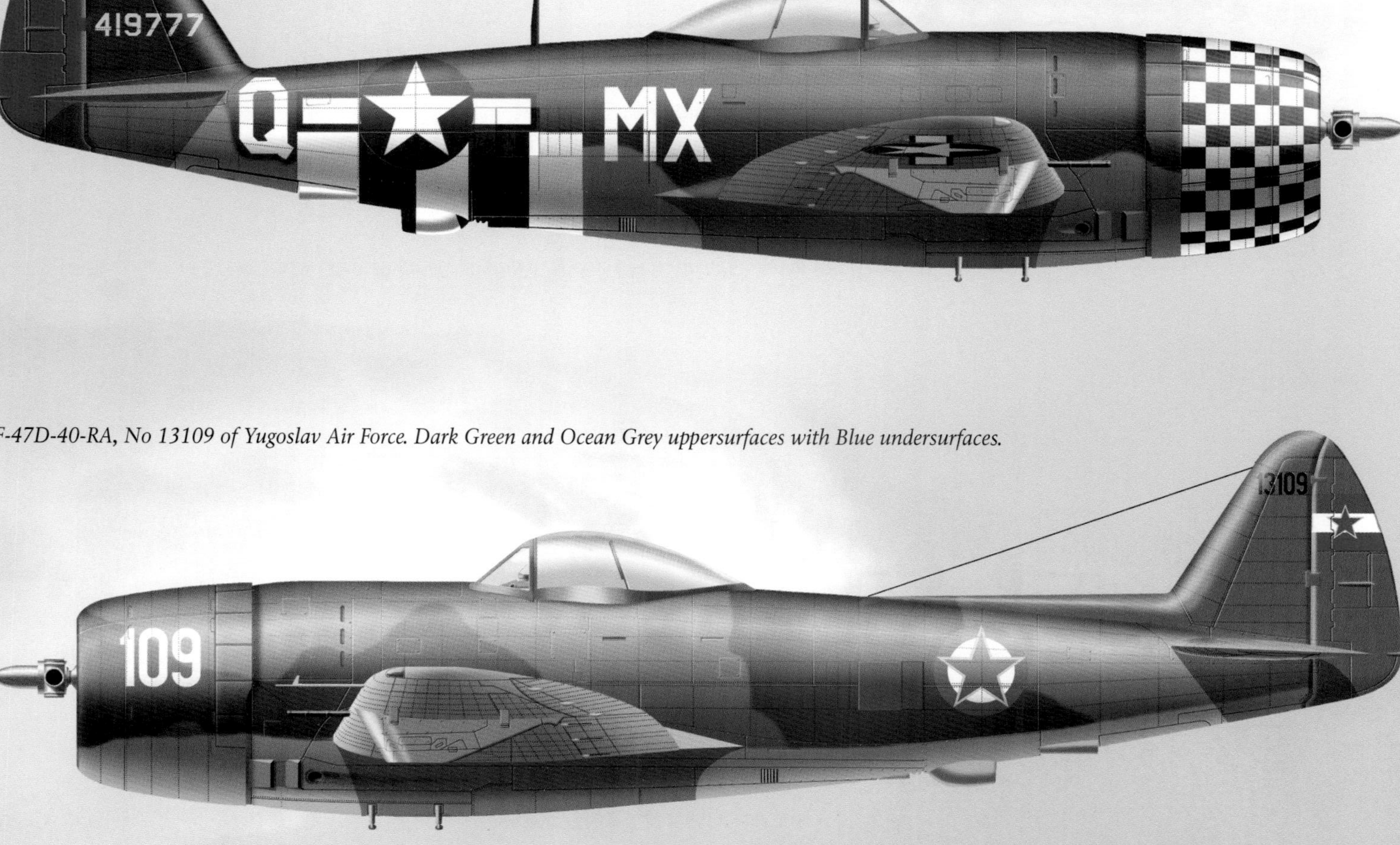

P-47D-28-RE, serial 44-19777, MX-Q of 82nd FS, 78th FG. Aircraft used by Edwin F. Bolgert and Donald C. Hart. Dark Green upper surfaces and Sky undersurfacess.

F-47D-40-RA, No 13109 of Yugoslav Air Force. Dark Green and Ocean Grey uppersurfaces with Blue undersurfaces.

P-47D-30-RA, serial 44-32710 of 1st Air Commando Group, CBI Theatre. Natural metal overall.

P-47D-30-RE, serial 44-21055, "G9-E" of 509th FS, 405th FG, spring 1945. Aircraft Natural metal overall.

Melsbroek Airfield, Belgium, spring 1945. Personal aircraft of Howard M. Park. Natural metal overall.

P-47N-5-RE, serial 44-88689 of 456th FS, 414th FG, Iwo Jima, 1945. Natural metal overall.

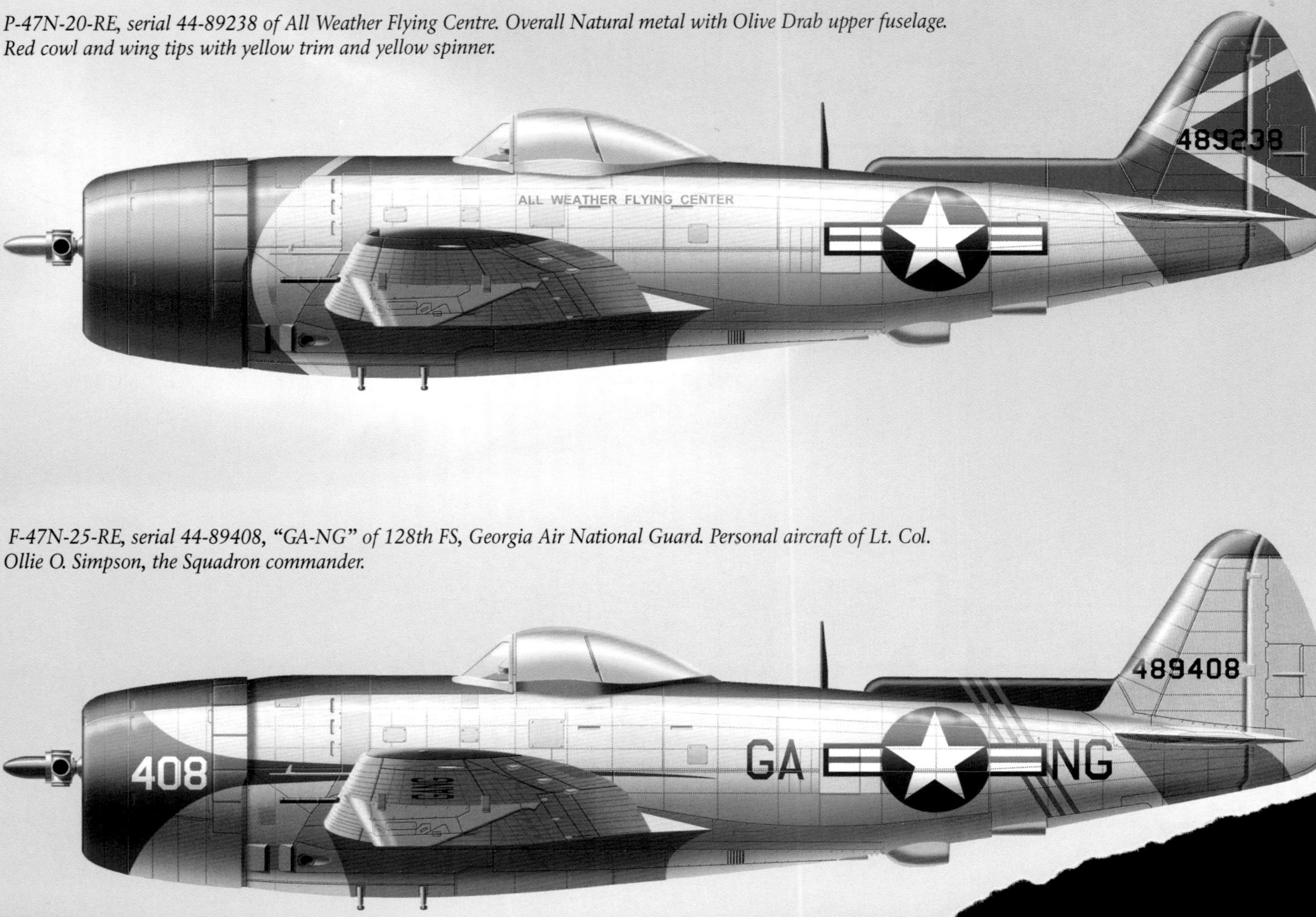

P-47N-20-RE, serial 44-89238 of All Weather Flying Centre. Overall Natural metal with Olive Drab upper fuselage. Red cowl and wing tips with yellow trim and yellow spinner.

F-47N-25-RE, serial 44-89408, "GA-NG" of 128th FS, Georgia Air National Guard. Personal aircraft of Lt. Col. Ollie O. Simpson, the Squadron commander.